ICE ON A HOT STOVE
A Decade of Converse MFA Poetry

Edited by
Denise Duhamel
and Rick Mulkey

Clemson-Converse Literature Series

In partnership with the Converse College Low Residency MFA program, the Clemson-Converse Literature series publishes a diverse and distinguished body of contemporary poetry, short fiction, and creative nonfiction essay collections. While the series will occasionally feature an outstanding anthology, the majority of the books will be selected through two competitions, each of which will run biennially: a national poetry prize for a full-length book, an award open to all poets publishing in English; and the Converse MFA Alumni Award series, open to students or alumni of the Converse Low Residency MFA.

ICE ON A HOT STOVE
A Decade of Converse MFA Poetry

EDITED BY
DENISE DUHAMEL
AND RICK MULKEY

Layout and design © 2021 Clemson University

Copyright of the poems remains with the authors.

Published by Clemson University Press, 116 Sigma Dr., Clemson, SC 29634

ISBN 978-1-63804-004-0

Typeset by Jae Dyche.
Cover image by Andrew Blanchard.
Cover design by Lindsay Scott.

Contents

INTRODUCTION   xi

ALBERT GOLDBARTH
- 1   Shawl
- 2   The Craft Lecture to the CreativeWriters of the Low-Residency Program at Yadda Yadda University, with a Late Assist from Wallace Stevens, Robert Frost, Maxine Kumin, Sir Thomas Browne, and Allusion to the Title of an Early Book of Jorie Graham's

CLAIRE BATEMAN
- 7   The Sinking of the Library
- 8   Blink
- 13   *A Pocket Introduction to Our Universe*
- 15   Mystique Academy
- 16   *The Index of Dead Brides*

DORIANNE LAUX
- 18   Lord Of The Flies
- 19   Souvenirs
- 20   Honeymoon
- 21   Joy
- 22   If It Weren't For Bad Ideas, I'd Have No Ideas At All

LILITH MAE McFARLIN
- 23   Total Eclipse of Eileen
- 26   Pussy Breath
- 28   I Don't Like Teriyaki Slim Jims

SUZANNE CLEARY
- 30   Sausage Candle
- 31   Dubbing Room
- 33   Asking for Breakfast
- 34   Elm Street

	35	Pascal's Wager
	37	Cheese-of-the-Month Club
RICK MULKEY	39	Cheese
	40	Cured
	42	Hunger Ghazal
	43	Blind-Sided
	45	Why I Believe in Angels
	46	Tool Box
	47	Cheerleaders at Forty
KATHLEEN NALLEY	48	Black Dress
	50	Concentric
	51	After the Layoffs
	53	Slow Churn
	55	The 49's
ASHLEY M. JONES	57	All Y'All Really from Alabama
	58	Slurret
	59	Love Note: Surely
	60	Contrapuntal with Gladys Knight and Infidelity
	61	Photosynthesis
	63	Harriette Winslow and Aunt Rachel Clean Collard Greens on Prime Time Television
GABRIELLE BRANT FREEMAN	65	Letters to Ted Allen
	66	In the Turn
	68	Girltrap
	70	Freak
	72	The Happily Married Woman Boards the Plane
DENISE DUHAMEL	73	How It Will End
	75	How Much Is This Poem Going To Cost Me?

	77	On The Occasion of Typing My First Email on a Brand New Phone
	79	Egg Rolls
	81	Howl
LISA HASE-JACKSON	82	Just
	84	You Find Yourself in Kansas City
	85	Yield
	86	33rd and Southwest Trafficway
	87	Shard Studded Floor
	88	Junk Mail
TYREE DAYE	89	When My Mother Had the World on Her Mind, Crickets in Her Ear
	90	Ready
	91	Tamed
	92	Same Oaks, Same Year
	93	Gin River
	94	Dirt Cakes
MELISSA DICKSON JACKSON	95	Ode to the Avocado
	96	The Mermen Of Forsyth Park
	97	Paper Bird
	98	Diorama
	99	The Humans
	100	Taking the Backroads to the Orthodontist
DAVID COLODNEY	102	Glass
	103	Turnstiles
	104	Passengers
	105	Reserved
	106	Deployed
SARAH COOPER	107	Pantoum for Departing
	108	Centered

	109	Hands & Mouth
	110	Hiking with an Erasure Heart after Adrienne Rich's "The Floating Poem, Unnumbered" & years of Emily Dickinson & Sappho
	111	Driving Home
	112	As a carpenter's daughter
JUAN J. MORALES	113	My Father Looking at Bruegel's *Landscape With The Fall Of Icarus*
	114	Like a Tired Balloon
	115	Dog Eats Hand
	116	The Democracy of John Elway
	117	Pueblo Boulevard Elegy
	118	Every Last Supper
ZORAIDA ZIGGY PASTOR	119	Salami and Cucumbers
	120	Late Night
	121	My Mother's Tongue
	122	You Bring out the Cubana in Me
	124	Fire
RICHARD TILLINGHAST	125	I Tuned Up Seán's Guitar
	126	The Boar
	129	Blue If Only I Could Tell You
	131	Or
	132	Took My Diamond to the Pawnshop
	133	Leavetaking
JULIE MARIE WADE	134	Atlantic Elegy
	136	In Perpetuity, I Shall Remain the Question My Parents Guess Wrong on *Jeopardy!*
	138	What Date Rape and Gay Marriage Have in Common
	140	Psalm in the Spirit of an Inaugural Poem

GARY JACKSON	144	After the Reading
	146	Elegy that was already done before
	147	Homecoming
	148	Fiat Lux
	149	Graduation
	150	You can't write poetry about things that happened a week ago
ACKNOWLEDGMENTS	151	
CONTRIBUTORS	155	

Introduction

Robert Frost discussing poetry once wrote, "Like a piece of ice on a hot stove the poem must ride on its own melting." To suggest the poems in this anthology ride on their own melting is not far-fetched. The poets collected here, all core faculty, visiting faculty, and alumni of the Converse College Low Residency MFA poetry program, to be sure recognize the many traditions in which their poems exist, something readers might expect from writers connected to an academic writing program. Yet, each poet acknowledges that tradition is not the same as creation. While the reader will find sonnets, villanelles, pantoums, elegies, odes, and plenty of free verse poetry, these pieces and their poets challenge expectations of form, music, subject, gender, race, politics, and class, and often challenge us as readers. Ultimately, as editors, we hope you will be as exhilarated by the ride on that melting ice as we have been when reading these poems.

Beyond representing the state of American poetry in general, this collection is meant to bring together a very specific group of poets, those associated with the Converse College MFA program from a single decade, 2009-2019. In addition, given that so many of these authors, while not all native to the area, currently live in North Carolina or South Carolina, or in additional Southeast states, it also serves as a snapshot of the poetry of this region. Each writer included in the anthology has contributed to the Converse community. All of these writers, including the alumni, have published at least one book, and many are award-winning authors of multiple collections selected or nominated for such prizes as the National Book Critics Circle Award, the National Book Award, the Cave Canem Poetry Prize, the Hillary-Tham Collection, the Bryant-Lisembee Editor's Prize, The APR/Honickman First Book Prize, and others.

Though the voices present in the anthology represent a single writing community, we think they are diverse and multi-layered, and our ordering of the poets in the anthology is meant to compliment that multiverse of personal, political, and poetic perspectives found in these poems. An alphabetical ordering simply didn't work for us—nor did the separation into sections of core faculty, visiting faculty, and alumni. We wanted to highlight back and forth conversations, the learning and the interplay that have been the hallmark of our MFA residencies. Still, we hope you will agree with us the writers all belong together. They may not be blood relatives, but they are certainly family, and we are pleased to present them to you as one means to enjoy the words, music, and lives of the Converse MFA community.

The Editors

Albert Goldbarth

Shawl

Eight hours by bus, and night
was on them. He could see himself now
in the window, see his head there with the country
running through it like a long thought made of steel and wheat.
Darkness outside; darkness in the bus—as if the sea
were dark and the belly of the whale were dark to match it.
He was twenty: of course his eyes returned, repeatedly,
to the knee of the woman two rows up: positioned so
occasional headlights struck it into life.
But more reliable was the book; he was discovering himself
to be among the tribe that reads. Now his, the only
overhead turned on. Now nothing else existed:
only him, and the book, and the light thrown over his shoulders
as luxuriously as a cashmere shawl.

The Craft Lecture to the Creative Writers of the Low-Residency Program at Yadda Yadda University, with a Late Assist from Wallace Stevens, Robert Frost, Maxine Kumin, Sir Thomas Browne, and Allusion to the Title of an Early Book of Jorie Graham's

Neoglyphea neocaledonica—nicknamed the "Jurassic shrimp"— was known only from 50-million-year-old fossils until a living specimen turned up in [2006]. NEW SCIENTIST

The Earth was writing: the Earth had penmanship.
That was my dream. I remember so little of it. I know
that hyenas and, after, pincer-beetles
had made a great clean whiteness, made a bone frond
ten feet long or more, of a giraffe's neck—and by this
I could see that the Earth was practicing cursives.
But the rest of it? ... a fizzle, another adventure
gathering think-dust on a back shelf
at the lost & found. I tell you,
keep a dream journal. Read, of course: read wide
and deep. Revise. Be open. And keep
a dream journal, and keep it
handy, and keep it a continent of vacant clay
that requires your staked-out cities. It was dawn,
or almost-dawn, it was the hind tit of night.
My father was telling me ... what? A stick of wisdom
from his pocket package of gum? a joke? a picture of what
it's like to be the new guy at the daily meeting of dead men
and to have to admit you're still addicted
to living? ... he was telling me ... but then it was moss,
and then it was a molecular architectural sketch of moss,
and then it was nothing. Keep a dream journal.
Keep it a vast and empty snow
that requires your skitter of tracks: your alphabet. Be rapid
and accurate. Audubon needed to work his birds
immediately onto a page, if the color were going to be true
to the throbbing picante of life, for if he waited ... the viridian,
the flame-blue, all of the telegraphed dabs of ruby among the saffron tufts
or even the definition under coal-fleck gray,
would drain away with the blood,
the now; so keep a dream journal. Keep it adhesive,
awaiting the touch of a flange of the dream,

a fin, a nylon, a bee of the dream
to innocently nuzzle against the stickiness
and be fastened. Otherwise, every new awaking
is an alzheimer's of the preceding eight hours,
their civilizations' temples and faro palaces get buried
under jungle vine and tundra grass
and the vortex of worry and passion that constitute ongoing life;
and the nightly hundred roanokes,
the thousand amelia earharts ... only crumbs
a fresh day brushes off into oblivion. This is my shtick
and my stump-speech exhortation to you, delivered in spittle
and neural knotways: keep a dream journal.
Research. Hobnob ["network"] ["shmooze around"].
And keep a dream journal, and keep it
open expectantly at your bedside, in the battle against ephemerality.
Lordy what did *these* notes once suggest as a promise—*Pizza to Priesthood*,
another, *Kowtowing in Cowtown*. Now they may as well be the nodes
and the squirms and the toadstool caps of Easter Island script,
they may as well be the impossible fogbound news
that once—but *really*, it couldn't be, *could* it?—
we walked on the moon. It was the ink of night,
the ebony ceiling of night, and my mother was saying
we can witness the internal undoing
of sixteenth-century oil paintings sometimes on an annual basis
—sometimes even daily, as a face is increasingly veiled
in an ever-finer mesh of subtle chemical degrading; for example,
the face of the infant Christ becomes a bag, a net bag
with a rosebud pout of a closure, that dangles from Mary's arm as she
sits surrounded by shepherds.... My *mother*
said that? Well, no. She said that she was dead,
somewhere inside my head, but speaking with the soft eyes
and the wry tilt of a parakeet (from my childhood? *that* one?)
lecturing on the passing of all things earthly, and she told me
to tell you to keep a dream journal, to keep it
for her, so she would have a place to land
after flying all night until sunrise. Save the mothers:
keep a dream journal. Save the ancient sky observatories
from sinking under carpets of creeper and kudzu.
A few of them rise up on their own and wink
in the sun for a moment—Atlantis of course is frequently
coquettish that way—but cities and even dynasties
are no more stable than gleam in an eye; and, as we know,
our own childhoods can't be fully dredged to the surface light
by the derring-do of the surest divers, so even if it's the nearest
wad of bar receipts or burger-blearied napkins, I adjure you

to note there mightily (and accurately), oh I adjure you
to keep a dream journal, I claim you as duly deputized
into that order. And when the curator lifted the jar with the thing
inside chat looked like a shrunken, salted
catcher's-mitt-with-a-rat-tail-wrapped-as-elegantly-as-one-
of-Cleopatra's-silver-armlets-around-it ... that
was a save, a dream journal, so was the jar
with the thing that looked like a star from a child's picture book
(only fallen to earth, so dwindled in size of course, but glorified
in falling, the way that Icarus was, or Satan). These
have been lost: Etruscan; Borneo's Kelabit megalith writing;
and a thousand of others of what were "living tongues"
and had the living day on their muscular, moist, exploratory tips
—their braggadocio: gone, their adulatory paeans to their gods,
and their most sniveling whinings: ditto, their chanties
and lullabyes and war cries and whatever was their oh-oh-oh
of flesh-on-flesh and sexual dew: all, gone.
How many species gone?—a footprint of some dinosaurs could serve
as a hotel wading pool, while others could fit in a plover's egg,
and all of them: gone. A spatula and a glove
are lost, were dropped by the space shuttle crew, and now
the one is almost grabbing hold of the other, forever, up there
in some mystery orbit. "Prosopagnosia": tragic
inability to recognize faces: after a virus
caused an inflammation in her temporal lobe, one mother of four
"can't recognize the faces of her children, her husband,
or even herself." And what I said in 1975 to make Sylvia
weep so?—gone. All of my past lives—gone, the one
in which I slew the enemy host,
the one in which I wore a porkpie hat
and mooched off relatives—gone, the pogroms of time
have made a thinning silt of these. And your innocence?—lost.
(I think I saw it looking like the star in a children's picture book,
but cinders now.) And any reclamation of these
would be a marvel worthy of a dream journal. There are blazons
to be notched on the trail going back. If you see my mother or father
in *your* dreams, write them down—be gentle, as they would be
with you—and then check the identification bands I've cinched
in one of my dreams around their wrists, and give me a call
to tell me how far they've traveled. These have been found:
The earliest dental work from the Americas,
4,500 years old—these teeth the color by now

of supermarket curry, that were ground down so
that they could be mounted with panther or wolf teeth.
Water on Mars. Rivets from the *Titanic*. A face
that was drawn in a cave on calcite 27,000 years ago.
Numerous pieces of chicken from the uterus
of a fifty-year-old woman in Finland (she believed that
"they would grow into a baby"). DNA, farmed from the tooth
of a Neanderthal child discovered in a Belgian cave.
Your high school yearbook. Something under the bed
that doesn't require detailing here, except to point out
water on Mars was far more likely. All of these
instances of conservancy score an *oh wow* on the aura-meter.
Reclaim the forsaken. Work, of course, on your resumé,
on keepin' up, on gettin' down—and think of Viktor Sarianidi:
"No one believed that anyone lived here until I came!";
(*here* being the harsh steppe-desert land of what today
is Turkmenistan) and yes, in fact "Most scholars had thought
that such sophisticated settlements hadn't taken root
in the region until 1,000 years later or more" than Sarianidi proved;
but he had a dream; and he spent thirty years at digs where sometimes
plagues of locusts "filled the trenches faster
than they could be shoveled"; still, he shoveled; in heat
that shovel-whacked straight back at him, and under the threat
of occupying military forces, he chiseled determinedly; and now
indeed we have this further feather in the cap
of our human accomplishments, and from its smallest
artifacts—a silver clothing pin in the shape of a camel
(the point ascending from one of its humps), a three-inch sturgeon
shaped of bronze (with a comical face that could pass
for a parrot's) —we can move up to the scale
of the central citadel and its towers, here in the town of Gonur
from 4,000 years in our past, its orchard canals
with glacier-fed water, its gold and ivory trade routes,
and its elaborate graves complete with wheeled carts
to roll in service along the avenues of the afterlife,
and from these we can move to a world implied beyond
the physical evidence: of theology and metallurgical expertise,
and the agri-lore for lentil and barley, and gender roles,
and the philosophical bullshit-swapping late into the night:
as amazing as water on Mars: another, earlier Earth
inside the earth: another planet really, only

cognate with ours: and the everyday carnelian brooches
and lapus lazuli figures of somebody's version of Irving
and Fannie Goldbarth is entered now in this registry that keeps
it all from going up with the kindling: hoe,
I tell you, the rows of your dream journal. Just the other day I heard
someone say "hooliganism," someone said "prie dieu," they
grabbed these words by the collar just as they were about to fall
off the edge of the map of the recognizable universe. Keep
your own preserve, and keep it pluripotent. Husband
its brawn. What *did* it mean when I dreamed
of a sexy new cop for a TV show, named Rachel Profiling?
—Keep a dream journal. Obviously Proust did
in between the lecture circuit and the interviews: a folio-dimensioned,
moleskin-bound affair with gilt-and-deckled edges.
Dickinson's: straight, square, satin-black; when she was done
for the day with her letters to public relations agencies,
she would add to its pages by the light of a single candle
as alabaster and gently numinous as an Easter lily. Famously,
Bukowski's was a bright pink, with a rainbow appliqué
on top and a teensie heart-shaped lock to keep it private.
Keep it. Daily attend to it. We are as butter
under the summer sun. The only emperor *is*
the emperor of ice cream. Tempus fugit. The woods
are lovely, dark and deep. I tell you all of our residency
is low residency. Our ground time here will be brief.
We start with "eros," but add a single final "ion" and
we're crumbling away at the continental rim. I tell you
nothing is more dust than a mountain, no matter
its seemingly imperturbable bulk. Therefore
it cannot be long before we lie down in darkness,
and have our light in ashes. Hail, rust. Hello
to the waves of video blahblahblah erasing hi$t$ory.
When my colleague Don the Shakespeare expert retires
he will not be replaced. *Shakespeare*: not replaced. Now
he will wither at the petal, he will feel the ravening worm
in the very kernel. Last night my childhood knocked
for attention against the inside of my cranium,
a ten-year-old boy and a hazy duo behind him looking
as if he could never grow up to fail or disappoint,
I heard them say that memory is holy, and nothing
—not the son or the Son or the sun overhead itself—is eternal.
Keep a dream journal.

Claire Bateman

The Sinking of the Library

It's true I once lived in The Library, though for how long I couldn't say, since time there eddied in chronological densities and expansions the reference librarian tracked through the stacks by radar light.

And it's true I was "unofficial." Ever the lone leaper, I, and a girl as well, I'd never sought initiation into the Noble Confederacy of Stowaways, but instead had stolen passage on my own. There in my hiding-place among the gears and pistons I was the first to hear—in the overlapping echoes of the Library's respiration—that slight, nearly inaudible ping signaling fracture. And this is also true: fast as I climbed through the ventilation system, I was so far behind everyone else who was fleeing that when I emerged from the duct, I found myself—oh wonder!—completely alone as the great vessel creaked and groaned toward rupture. Just as the prophecies had foretold, the Library was disgorging itself, never again to receive a group on pilgrimage.

So I was the last one to see the pneumatic tubes where a covey of languid documents were still undergoing the flight treatment, visible only as a spectral blur through glass, but I did not pause to release them. I was the last to see the combustion wing where asbestos-gloved professionals had been "milking" the flames from between the pages of perpetually burning books. Seeking escape, these staff members had abandoned the volumes to their agonizing fullness, but I stopped my ears against their cries and ran on, passing the recreation deck where only moments ago, a pilgrim had been reading aloud to selected periodicals. The Library winds were ripping themselves apart. I had to keep moving.

As I sped through the stacks, I beheld the texts straining at their stations—books whose pages bled incense and oil, honey and milk; books bruised and trembling, chanting and murmuring, self-illuminating and self-occluding. Soon they would surge around me, beating the air on their stampede to be ingested by the earth or packed into glacial salt. Or they would wander the globe in swarms, moult in mountain aeries, congregate on the ocean floor as a vast and rising reef of bibliocadavers.

What would they then have in common? Only their illegibility. And since everyone else who had been on board perished in the sea, I am the only witness to the close of the Library Age, which set the world free to become The Book of the New Unread.

But it isn't completely true that I rescued nothing. At the final instant, a book flew into my arms as if of its own accord, and I rode it out over the waves, for its sheer black opal page was strangely buoyant.

This was The Book of Refreshment that cleanses the mind so you can read the same tale again and again for the very first time.

Blink

Everyone was writing a dystopian novel,

and everyone had a podcast or at least a blog,

and every phrase that seemed like a good band name

turned out to be a band name already,

and the punishment for information

was more information, as was the reward,

and through almost an entire week,

real-time images of an actual black hole

scintillated around the globe

while we debated the particulars of attribution,

and we were all incompatibly lonely

as we outsourced our disambiguation,

each of us gazing into a palmed incandescence

instead of the starry heavens above

or the reeking entrails of gutted sheep,

and every time we bought groceries

we re-titrated the degree of toxins

we were willing to ingest,

but there were still pockets of local solace

scattered amidst the impending,

so it was possible to savor sushi

on the same day you declined to discard

an unfinished bottle of Tramadol—

how long would analgesics be available?—

and because we were ever more achingly cognizant

of the textured, fretted, speckled, tender underside of things,

art was either prophetic elegy or elegiac prophecy,

and for some of us, the projected time of collapse

corresponded to our own natural end,

though *Will I still be alive when the world is over?*

asked the nine-year-old as his mother marked

his birthday inches on the wall,

and in speaking of our situation there was social protocol

which consisted of reticence and restraint,

though sequence continued to coexist with simultaneity,

and the Lost and Found ceased not its overflow,

and newborns persevered in the struggle

to inhabit their own flailing,

and the young continued shining unaware,

and breath still wandered through our bodies

like a wickless flame,

everything no less unlikely and irreducible

in this dense serendipitous connotative clumpy world

clotted with decisions we hadn't noticed

until we found ourselves together on the other side,

and what was that just barely within our audible range,

the sound of events becoming retroactively inevitable,

or had we failed to notice

a single moment of no-taking-back,

when the nascent future flew out,

slick, new-hatched, through a chink, a crack,

a fissure, the proverbially yawning gap?

Now there we were moving swiftly,

no, suspended inside a momentum

whose shape we could not trace,

and all the algorithms were about

how we were more the same than different,

more different than the same,

and our pre-extinction consciousness

was just as inaccessible

as our pre-digital consciousness,

and any soul aspiring to reincarnate

would have to aim for someplace in the past—

how crowded it would be with multitudes

crammed into each of the much fewer

available human bodies back in the day!—

but were we, as a species, old or young?

Wasn't it only recently we'd all nestled

in the center of celestial crystalline spheres?

Now that which had been submerged was rising up,

and that which had stood high was going under,

and the little ice chapel in Helsinki

was thawing at the same rate it evaporated,

and the leafy places of the earth were limned with flame,

so why hadn't the teams been deployed

 to peel away all the shadows, fold them tenderly

for cold storage lest they warp and scald?

Now the simplest of greetings meant,

Are we still here?

like children waking up through the night,

tiptoeing to the window to see if it's snowing.

A Pocket Introduction to Our Universe

What does our universe most like to do?

To contort without any warning
into nothing but corners,
an awkward though not unbeautiful
configuration.

Of what elements is our universe composed?

The first is distance,
of which there are innumerable varieties,
such as the chromatic stutter between
forethought and aftertaste,
and the measureless span between
the transparent and the merely translucent.

The second is otherness,
that of the other
and that of the self,
reciprocal and ever-escalating glories.

What holds things together and apart?

The strong and weak gravitational forces.
Scar tissue.
The Great Universal Loneliness,
from which not even the material realm
has been excluded.

What are some of the forces that pass through flesh and bone?

Neutrinos.
X-Rays.
Invisibility itself passes through the body
in immense, inarticulate storms.

What are some of the anomalies of our universe?

Holes may be filled but never undug,
and may perish by suffocation or drowning,
but never suicide.

A small sadness may easily dislodge
a larger one.

We have fireproof gloves,
but not gloves of flame,
which surely could be of use.

What in our universe can be trusted?

The perpetual transformation
of inside into outside,
and vice versa.

Anything so damaged
it can suffer
no further harm.

Anything so far fallen
it has nowhere deeper
to go.

What is the primary mode of light and matter?

Unappeasable deference and displacement:
"After you!"
"No, no, I insist; after you!"

What was time contemplating as it sprang into existence?

Thirst and the water of drinking fountains,
their common surge —
ever too much
before it becomes enough.

Mystique Academy

The first thing they taught us is that hair isn't dead.
An exotic state of matter, it's composed primarily of discontinuities, retracting at an average rate of a quarter-inch a month.
We learned that a child may become tearful or agitated on the occasion of its first hair-lengthening, and how to distract it.
We learned to identify and respond to the singular tone each follicle emits as we chant out the strands that yearn to hide in cognitive obscurity.
We committed to memory the esoteric names of the various knots, tangles, and convolutions we'd encounter.
We were examined on the circumstances under which the separate emptiness of those knots' vital cores might, without our intervention, first stellify and then opacify into spinning inversions.
We were tested in dim rooms and assessed in a harrowing glare; we were questioned underwater and tried in our sleep.
And don't we now tremble at our stations, wielding the sacred torches on behalf of those whose hair is finally long enough for apotheosis?
There's nothing more paradoxical than our work—red burns the slowest, then blonde and brown.
But black goes up in a flash, as though darkness excites the flame.

The Index of Dead Brides

is an appallingly cheerful read.
Like the TV police detective
due to retire within the week,
each of these brides
had been unable to ignore the fact
that she was, archetypically,
a sitting duck; thus, the proverbial
dropping of the (white satin) shoe
came to all of them
as something of a relief.
Invisible to the naked eye,
they may now be located
through gown spectography,
except for the peat bog bride
who died clad in rope and starlight.
Rendered by death
permanently immune to death,
and immune to nostalgia
by the recent pandemic
of dead-bride amnesia,
the rest of them
hang mothballed in the hall closet;
lounge sudsily in the bathtub;
slump in the driver's seat of the John Deere run amok;
proffer the parade wave, enthroned on the hundred-petticoated float;
taint the well water at the aquifer's throat.
Dead brides with their punctured pleura,
their caved-in clavicles,
their fractured femurs,
beauties who died iridescent,
who died intestate,
who died alone,
and so remain, except for
the mud-wrestling brides
rending each others' satin seams;
the brides anteing up around the card table
in veils and green eye shades,

like poker-playing pooches
(and are they not our pets,
pets of the world?);
and the bevy of brides
hurled throughout history
to the wolves—
these last, after having located each other
by the pitch of their human howling,
hitched up their silks
and began to lope in a pack,
less for the sake of the speed itself
than for the solidarity
found therein.

Dorianne Laux

Lord of the Flies

"Coronavirus Conference Gets Canceled Because of Coronavirus."
—*Bloomberg News, March 10, 2020*

I can already see the streets
filling with corpses piled
tenderly along the curbs.

First the homeless, then
the poor, then those who
were lost, depressed, lonely,

alone. The rich will be last,
top of the pile as they were
in life. Dressed in their finery.

Oh the ball gown shrouds.
The worthless pearls.

Souvenirs

I brought you this chocolate in gold foil
shaped like a mandolin, pregnant
with song. I brought you this black
music box that plays Clare de Lune,
this Sachertorte, these naughty
Mozart balls with crushed green
pistachio nut cores, this pocked
porcelain thimble, this snow globe
with its sealed mixture of glycerin
and glycol, also known as antifreeze.
I brought you these Viennese trees,
which are no different than American trees
except they are Viennese, these three
clouds caught on the spire of Saint
Stephen's Cathedral, stuffed
into a blue jam jar. I brought you
the scent of horse dung drifting
through an open window, the cries
of the couple next door
who rubbed their bodies together,
a swan and a lark, two violins in the dark.

Honeymoon

We didn't have one, unless you count Paris,
20 years later, after we'd almost given up on the idea.
We'd imagined one, long nights beneath
a warm celestial sky, him growing his beard,
me in a silk turquoise robe, floating, billowing,
on a deserted beach foraging for whole sand dollars,
jelly fish washed up on the shore, their glittering insides
visible, still pulsing through flesh made of glass,
but it never happened. We had to work through
our vacations, refinance the house, find someone
to cut down the cedar that threatened to bury us
with each storm. We wanted to make up
for the wedding, or lack of one, the granite
courthouse steps, the small room with a desk,
the flimsy document stamped with a cheap gold seal.
Even then we meant to have a party on the deck,
cheese and crackers, fruit plates, sparkling
grape cider in plastic cups, our friends on the lawn
calling you the Big Kahuna, me Mrs. Dynamite,
me calling you my Sweet Dragon, you calling me
your Little Red Corvette. Instead, time found a way
to demand each minute, until one night,
after you'd gotten a small windfall in the mail,
you turned to me and said, *I'm going to take you to Paris*,
me in my ratty robe and floppy slippers, you
in your flannel PJ bottoms and black wife beater,
muting the clicker when I said "What?"
and saying it again. Then we were there,
in our 60's, standing below the dire Eiffel Tower,
its 81 stories of staircases we couldn't possibly climb,
its 73 thousand tons of puddled iron, you
taking my picture for posterity, me
kissing you beneath the pathway of arched trees,
our voices echoing against the six million skulls
embedded in the stone Catacombs, me
saying *I guess you weren't kidding*, you
taking my hand in the rain.

Joy

Even when the gods have driven you
from your home, your friends, the tree
you planted brought down by storm,
drought, chain saw, beetles, even

when you've been scrubbed
hollow by confusion, loss,
accept joy, those unbidden
moments of surcease--

the quiet unfolding
around your shoulders
like a shawl, the warmth
that doesn't turn to burning.

When the itch has stopped, the cough,
the throb, the heart's steady beat
resumed, the barn door

open to the shade, the horse inside
waiting for your touch, apple
in your pocket pocked, riddled

the last to fall, the season
done. As you would accept
air into your lungs, without
thinking, not counting

each breath. As you accepted
the earth the first time you stood
up on it and it held you, how it was

just there, a solid miracle,
gravity something you would
learn about only later
and still be amazed.

If It Weren't for Bad Ideas, I'd Have No Ideas At All

A bad idea is like a road we go down
at dusk, passing each lit gas station
thinking it won't be the last, as if home
could be anywhere behind us, any grief
we don't need, like the chipped knife
in the glove box, the month of December
with its cold stars, its end-of-the-world trees.

We forget to pack a jacket, down or tweed:
no dinner parties, no search parties, just you
and your burning, your Big Because,
a boom beneath that could be a bald tire
giving up, the resonant sound in your brain
saying *Keep going, ride on the rims.*

Lilith Mae McFarlin

Total Eclipse of Eileen

I shouldn't be dating during a global pandemic,
but I'm American and I'm selfish and I want this now.
I put my mask on—the one with the skull across the front.

I walk into the bar where a guy stamps my hand;
it's in the shape of a Mickey Mouse glove giving the finger.

I wanted to go to a coffee shop,
but she insisted on this Budweiser-stained dive,
even though I barely drink enough to write about it these days.

I order my signature neat double bourbon,
and the bartender pours enough whiskey in my glass
to drown a hundred rednecks.
I can practically see their cowboy hats
floating at the top.

I just need a little booze
to melt the rocks in my stomach.
Anything more than ninety-nine drowning rednecks
is reserved for hearts breaking
like dropped high ball glasses,
not hair twirling around the fingers of anxiety.

I look all over for my date,
then I realize the stage is in the backroom,
and we wanted to go to karaoke night.

If you're queer in the south and
want to meet someone new,
you have to drive to the next town over
while mosquito guts rain on your windshield.

She's not in the backroom either,
but I'm on time for once, so I wait.

Even this anxiety is a privilege
because I have a job right now.
As a white woman,

on the off-chance a police officer broke through
my front door like it was a crumbling cracker and
shot my sleeping body,

he would be arrested for murder,
unlike Brett Hankison, Myles Cosgrove, and Jonathan Mattingly
who murdered ed Breonna Taylor.

But at least someone important might read this.

Two sips of bourbon smolder down my timid throat
drop by drop
because I haven't had a shot since
the mosquitos woke up last Spring.

People stumble through the entryway,
and not one of them is my fucking date.
After my third sip,
they stagger the opposite way
to lay puking across the backseat of an Uber.

I make a face and decide to quit drinking for now.
A guy steps up to the karaoke machine
and slurs to the tune of "Total Eclipse of the Heart,"
but the lyrics slobbering out of his mouth
are from "Come on, Eileen."
That feels about right.

I've texted my date five times,
to no response.
This is worse than that time someone
only went out with me
to sell pictures of my feet.

I think of how she said she identifies as "questioning,"
and I wonder if she hasn't even
touched someone else's boob for the first time.

Hell, I'm used to making out
in places like this by now.

She might be embarrassed to be seen on a date
with another woman—
let alone one that is trans.

Why did I drive all this way for someone
who might could be a ghost?
All we talked about was our favorite Ramones albums.

And fuck her,
Rocket to Russia will always be better
than Road to Ruin.

We also discussed how long I've been on estrogen;
the fact that I'm still pre-op.

I usually tell people that before the first date
so I don't waste my time.
She's not coming.

My face feels redder than a hot stove.

So I text her,
"This has never happened to me before.
I hope things happen to you that make
the most seasoned professional
rip their hair out and
run all the way to Argentina."

I instantly follow-up with an apology.
That was too far.

I'm American and I'm selfish and I wanted this.
But no one always gets what they want,
and we owe each other nothing—
not even basic kindness, apparently.

Half the people in here aren't even wearing masks.
I can at least have this:
for once, I didn't fuck on the first date.
That's so classy.

Pussy Breath

I'm tired of being just coffee in someone's mug,
where the last sip is always gone too soon.
Even though there is often a whole pot,
and you can enjoy it for hours—
        I am a stallion.

There's a bra beneath my coffee table.
I'm almost sure of who it belongs to.
It's too lacy, frilly, and floral to be mine,
and I'm not galloping away with her again.

How she lay against me with her head on my breasts
for forty-five minutes;
how I eventually kissed from her throat
all the way down;

how my thumb and two fingers sat cold and useless
in their stable like racing season was over;
how she felt me up underneath my bra
like we were in high school;

how I slept with her, even though she noticed my menorah,
then she asked me what it was for then what Chanukah was;
how long she let the spearmint
stay on my breath;

how she pulled me up by my hair,
then her cold hands on my bare back.

It's ten a.m. and my mug is empty
for the last time this morning.
My menorah is covered with dried-up wax
that was once melting down hot.
        Only in Arkansas would someone
        not know what Chanukah is.

We both went by Lily
and had the same blue dye job
and multiple ear piercings.

Now I have to ask myself if I'm going to keep fucking myself
with all these casual encounters because my reflection
is so similar to my mental image of her.

It's ten a.m. and my mug is empty
for probably the last time this morning.

I Don't Like Teriyaki Slim Jims

I'm driving a Camaro down the road and there's flames
painted on the sides of that motherfucker.
There's only one seat in that motherfucker
so I don't miss your
deliciously smoky, one-liner voice beside me.

Never mind, the passenger seat is there
and you've been replaced
by a motherfucking tiger
and I pet its head at stoplights while it purrs.

This kind of sad needs comfort snacks,
so I'm eating Slim Jims and I'm feeding
the teriyaki ones to my striped friend.
It's like being a kid and
drawing pinup girls in Church
between making eye contact with the pastor.

Then I absent-mindedly miss my turn,
and I drive by the bar where we played bingo.
It was hosted by a drag queen,
who at first looked like a floating wig
behind the spinning cage thing
that holds all the B-9s and 0-72s.

I realize the thrill of this ride is more like
the comically too-pale foundation on
The Fabulous Miss Velveeta Rotel's face
that oozed like stale cheese dip over
her smoker mouth and decades of showbiz eye bags.

The Chevrolet fantasy ends.
All that's left is just me in my bright green Honda,
arriving home from work after the first day
I didn't cry in the bathroom.

I park, then lock myself inside my apartment.

I'm standing in front of the mirror,
where I pull out the scissors.
My gay and my white trash come together
like a bald eagle flying so high
it blocks the motherfucking sun.
I slash my hair into an emotional distress mullet.
Because you didn't try to change my mind
when I said I couldn't do this anymore.

You just weakly said you were sad,
breaking the promise made not only
by your square jaw and your serious blue eyes;

but how you always kissed me
as soon as we woke up in the morning
when I look like a back-water possum;
how your hips rested my hands
like party barges on the lake;
how I told you I wished I had
a better body to give you,
and you said
you loved every part of me.

All that's left is my hair on the floor,
and Tabasco tears dribbling from my eyes.
I know I said I would never hurt you,
but everyone
says that.

Suzanne Cleary

Sausage Candle

> *[A]longtime Manhattan resident...*
> *Ms. [Fran] Lee advised radio*
> *and television audiences on household*
> *and consumer issues from the late 1940s*
> *until well into the '90s. Her purview*
> *ranged from cyclamates to asbestos*
> *to how to make a candle from a sausage*
> .
>
> **New York Times** obituary, February 19, 2010

S
t
i
c
k
a wick in a sausage
and light it, and you've got
a candle, its flame fed by fat,
not that you'd burn it
on your birthday cake,
not that you'd light two
and process to an altar,
not that you'd want one,
even a small one, flickering
over your romantic dinner.
But the sausage candle gives light.
The sausage candle gives light.
Think of the books you could read
by the light of that candle,
think of the dark passages it might,
given the chance, illuminate.
It is better to light one sausage
than to curse the darkness.
Imagine, for a moment, you dare
set a sausage candle
atop your cake, and
you close your eyes and you wish.
Think of the wishes you could make
if you weren't afraid of the ridiculous.

Dubbing Room
Sony Pictures Studio, Culver City, CA

We crowd into the small booth, stare out
        at the man kissing his arm, his mouth pressing
the back of his hand so his loose fist bobs

like the head of a baby, nursing, sucking
        with furious instinct, its whole body gulping
with pleasure, unlike this professional

whose pleasure we imagine the measured sigh
        of a job well done, this pucker and soft pull,
this wetting the lips precisely, so they will not chap

as he works, his one eye on the screen.
        Two actors clothed only in pink light
lie on a beach, their kisses falling short

of even the latest sound equipment, and so
        their kisses are supplied today, as we watch.
The tall, heavyset man wears a plaid shirt,

one sleeve rolled to the elbow.
        The kiss begins, it seems, not in his lips,
but in his hand, lips responding to the rise

and fall of his right hand, which he supports
        with his left, for control, or maybe for comfort,
to ease the ache in his right shoulder and the crook

of his neck, although he may court pain
        to inform these kisses, for the actors seem full
of sorrowful ardor—there, in the Pacific's rising tide.

He turns his hand over, now kissing the underside
        of his forearm, where the skin is petal-smooth.
I cannot turn away from him, despite the beautiful

lovers, twice life-size on the movie screen,
        embracing in the lapping water.
I stare at the man at the microphone,

who leans forward with something like tenderness,
        but both more and less than tenderness:
memory's enactment of love's keen attention.

He breathes deeply, slowly, makes small sounds
        in a language entirely spit and flesh.
In the soundproof booth, where we can say

anything, we stare and say nothing.
        If something is not real, does one feel
more intensely? Why can we say nothing,

not even to ourselves, as we watch
        what seems, although it is not,
what it would be to each love ourselves

and to stand thus before strangers,
        to roll up our sleeves
and, without fanfare or shame, get on with it?

Asking for Breakfast

One should live each day with the confidence
I displayed that day in Paris, when, at 4 p.m.,
I said to the waiter, *We would like to eat*

breakfast, if you please, exceedingly proud
of my accent, eager to demonstrate it again
for the white-haired waiter who raised

his dark eyebrows, requested I *repetez*.
He looked at my husband, then back at me,
and I like to think the waiter thought

I was boasting of our sex life, was suggesting
we had spent the day in bed, and not just
any day, but a day in Paris—

vendors polishing cages in the bird market
behind Notre Dame, shopkeepers in long aprons
washing sidewalks, well-dressed bureaucrats

riding bicycles, bouquets of flowers balanced
across the handlebars, as if they were in love
with the work ahead—that day, in bed.

I like to think we rose, then, in the waiter's esteem,
two Americans alive to the pleasures of the body,
and able to convey this information

with a sentence, although simple, stunningly
Gallic in subtlety: breakfast at the hour for tea.
But that day in Paris I thought not a whit

of the waiter's thought, not even as I caught
my mistake, and laughed, caught
my husband's amused, affectionate eyes.

That day in Paris, I gave not a flit of a thought
to the lonely table imagination sets. Hungry,
I asked for breakfast. I asked again.

Elm Street

I am so happy to see the man who lives in the house on the corner
        sit on the porch with a guitar on his knee, one arm draped
                loosely, as if he patiently scans a vast repertoire, choosing

which song to play, or as if he has stopped mid-song
        to tighten a string, then decided to listen to Elm Street
                and compose a new song, notes his fingers will find and follow,

for Elm Street is a steep hill that draws skateboarders like a magnet,
        that makes drivers roll down the truck window and stick an elbow out.
                Elm Street has been here since before it had a name, dirt path

from hilltop to river. I am happy if the man is new to the guitar, pauses
        in the middle of the only song he knows, because he has lost his place
                or lost touch with the touch he has learned to imitate, late nights

in his attic-room rental, this middle-aged man who works second-shift,
        home now for the night, which he will fill, perhaps, with song,
                or with stray notes that make song of the silence between them,

for sometimes song is beyond our reach, as found the art student
        who dutifully copied masterpieces until he saw his true gift: forgery.
                For a brief time, he built a life on copying Matisse,

for his simple line, unable to see that the line halted when the painter paused
        to look at his model. The line resumed with hesitance, a quaver
                the forger never could replicate, conceding,

I mastered his line, it was his pause I could not master—finally having seen
        that to see the model is to quaver in her presence, is to carry forward
                what little you can balance on the tip of the brush.

Silence, big silence that surrounds us, some of us dare to hear you.
        Tonight, I am happy it is the man on the corner, instead of me,
                who sits in your presence, and readies himself to play.

Pascal's Wager

Pascal's Wager is the kind of thing
you would discuss with a beer in your hand,
but then there was always a beer

in one of your hands, or passing from one to the other,
that summer we talked on your porch,
those rainy upstate nights, hot pavement steaming

as it cooled, the steam like fog close over a river,
beginning to lift toward invisibility.
I remember the wager like this: if we believe in God,

there is at least a chance we will see Heaven,
whereas, if we do not believe, we forfeit our place
in paradise. Pascal wrote there is no harm

in believing. If it turns out there is no God,
we've lost, he said, nothing, and if we do not believe,
and it turns out we are right, we have gained nothing,

Pascal not the kind of person, evidently,
to take satisfaction in having been right,
damned but right. I knew you drank. I saw the bottles.

I sat in your kitchen and I saw them, beside the stove.
You set your beer down to take a pot from the cupboard,
to pour rice into boiling water. You set it down again

to briefly admire, then chop, carrots and ginger,
to rinse red grapes, place them in a bowl,
all the while the two of us talking, a feast of ideas

and easy silence, as the small kitchen filled
with the smells of earth and, for all we knew,
for all we know, Heaven. When I think of you,

years later, it is usually because there is something
I want to tell you, or there is something I wonder about,
and I am alone in my wonder. I have thought

memory both Heaven and Hell. I wonder
if it is the same for you. Pascal's theology,
as I understand it, examines doubt

because he believes faith commodious beyond reason,
as is God, who has made earth our home,
and lets us mistake it for Heaven.

Cheese-of-the-Month Club

At first, it had seemed such a good idea,
        to open your home to the creamy, the crumbly,
the stinky, the blue, to open your home to this new life,
        the life where you open your mouth not to talk but to taste,
to find, the third Friday of every month, the box,
        heavy yet compact, its corrugated wings opening
onto another box, shiny and white, taped to its top
        a gold-edged card identifying the cheese by name and story,
to find at your door, dependably, a new reason
        to live in your body, to love your body:
the Venetian Pecorino, coated with black pepper
        providing a distinct bite with a little heat,
the Netherlands' Extra-Aged Farmer's Cheese, described as
        the dairy world's equivalent of a Rembrandt or VanGogh,
the description, true, sometimes a tad overripe, still,
        it seemed such a good idea to learn, to know, to savor
what at first you could barely discern, say,
        the Belgian Goat Cheese, *fruity, slightly herbed,*
its texture chalky yet creamy.
        What could this cheese not teach you
about contrast and balance, risk and poise?
        But now, each time you open the door, there is another cheese.
Now, Month Six, you doubt you can keep pace with it.
        It is likely to outrun you, even the cheese that is not runny,
even the aged cheese. You doubt your capacity for pleasure,
        your appetite for knowledge, your appetite itself. You doubt yourself worthy
of the gentle Buffalo-milk cheese called Bishop's Blessing.
        And how, by the way, does a month pass so quickly?
Do not ask for whom the cheese tolls. It tolls for thee,
        in Pomfret, Vermont, where a raw-milk organic cheese ripens
in one of the few copper cheese vats in the United States,
        a vat that, given the chance, would sing like a steel drum,
call everyone in Pomfret out into the street
        to dance in a long, swaying line,
except that you doubt people dance in the street in Vermont,
        where, it is said, there are two seasons: winter and roadwork.
Maybe you should live in Vermont, where nights are long and cold,
        where the cheese is mostly local, and you doubt people say much about it.
You doubt anyone would approve

   of the gold-edged card that boasts of *the subtle nut flavor,*
its complex finish redolent of a cove north of Pomfret.
   Redolent, you turn the word over with your tongue, your mind.
Redolent of a cove is enough to make you sign on for another year,
   for isn't this what you want, what you have always wanted,
to bite into life so deeply you can taste where it began?
   Isn't that desire what brought you here, somewhere south of Pomfret?

Rick Mulkey

Cheese

I'm not talking about the ones
threaded with veins of blue,
a living circulatory system of mold,
or the ones ripe with the pungency
of post-coital sweat. Those weren't for us.
Not then. I'm thinking of the big blocks
shaped like Egyptian mud bricks fashioned
with straw and blood, the ones
my father waited in line to receive
from the backs of trucks in that lean year,
 the strike year, the year of brown beans
and cornbread, the year when a hunk
of poorly aged cheddar toasted
between day old bread on a buttered griddle
was luxury beyond compare.
In those months my father stood
sign-in-hand in the picket line every day
asking for little more than his fair shake.
Every day, that is, except the first Thursday
of the month when he'd wait his turn
behind the welfare truck for powdered milk
and a block of processed American.
Cheese, even the way the vowels stretched
across the ear, the way it whispered the lie
of "ease" into the air sounded like shame.
Even now, sometimes a small gesture is all it takes.
The way my neighbor, Mr. Local-Big-Shot,
Mr. Raised-to-Take-Over-the-Family-Business,
Mr. My Way or the Highway,
eating aged Kobe beef for his 4th of July feast
piles a mound of Roquefort on his slightly rare,
and flirts with the caterer's assistant, a young Latina.
She hustles from guest-to-guest
with a quick smile, performing her obliging dance
of foot shuffle and head nod, hardly noticed,
and taking, when she thinks no one is watching,
a couple of hunks that the guests won't touch,
of the processed cheddar stabbed with a toothpick,
nibbling like a little mouse
around the edges of appetite.

CURED

for Albert Goldbarth

Albert, I'm here to tell you
Bluefield, Virginia has the best bacon
in the eastern U.S. I know
you've never been there, but it's the kind
of place you might visit on a Sunday,
clear blue sky and mountain ridges frosted,
when all the evangelicals in their aging
chapels and strip mall sanctuaries are off to pray
that folks like you and me won't turn
their fruitful lands into a salty waste,
and you'd be left alone
or nearly so, in the only diner
open on a Sunday morning. Just like me
you'd be lured in by the satisfying
aromas of peppered pork belly, the sensation
of eating the blistered fat of swine.
We wouldn't care that it was spiritually unclean,
or that all it touched was unclean,
the unclean plate, the unclean scrambled eggs,
the filthy toast and jam, the way our fingers
lathered in its fatty sweetness
were unclean, or our mouths unclean,
or the BLT we'd order to take
with us, piled high in bacon, unclean.
And later, as we walked the empty streets
before the local parishioners labored out
to find their way home to sanctified roasts
they'd ravage from pristine platters,
you and I and our friends would grow hungrier
and hungrier as we'd compare the subtle flavors
of acorn and truffle, the sugary-salty depth of pig.
Then you'd quote from Su Shi, Martial,
or Matthews' sensuous song of swine,
"Sooey Generous," and we'd agree that eventually
we'll all be offered up on one altar or another,
salted with fire and smoke, salted with age, salted
in baths, entering a covenant of salt, cured,
if you will, of any worries about what might
come to pass tomorrow. And knowing this life
is the one life and wanting to make the most of it,

we'd pick up a glass of very cold, very sweet tea
at the Dairy Queen, and we'd unwrap our sandwiches,
drink deeply from the cup, and eat of the crispy flesh,
satisfied celebrants of this porcine priesthood.

Hunger Ghazal

Even lonelier than the owl's question is the whisper of boiling water.
On the table, morning's cracked cup petitions its boiling water.

I wake to the root-bared light of November. While oaks shed
to reveal their truer selves, fog rises from my kettle of toiling water.

False summer, and the honeybee refuses the machinery of bloom and rot.
She sucks out life to form another: black tea transforming boiling water.

As a child, I saw rabbits after the flood spoil in the sun, crucified on briars
in creek side thickets. Empires of flies rose to profit beside the roiling water.

Of course there is the other, the teenage boy who spies the hips of housewives,
each daughters' sprouting breasts. Desire beaded on his lip, a kind of holy water.

My wife adds salted pork to the soup pot's steeped delicacies. Our hands brush gently,
as if again we're young lovers walking above the river's rolling water.

To look at us, you'd think we'd been happy all our lives. How much
our joy depends on love as bearable hunger, a pot of boiling water.

Blind-Sided

> *Only one person is known to have been hit by*
> *a meteorite. On November 30, 1954, Mrs. E.H. Hodges*
> *of Sylacauga, Alabama, was sitting in her house after*
> *lunch when a 9-pound stone crashed through the roof*
> *and hit her on the thigh.* —Walter Sullivan, *We Are Not Alone*

Nine years and three days later I drop to the earth
with considerably less speed, but with as great
an impact, or at least that's how my mother tells it.
And she lived to tell about it, as did Mrs. Hodges,
once she recovered from the shock, the thrill
of coming as close to the eternal universe, eternally,
as a few inches. But isn't that always the way.
One moment we're minding our own business,
wandering about in our lives, no apparent course,
the next we're rolling diapers into a meteoric knot
and hurling them into the pail.
Or, as with my friend J., we're finishing
our lunch when out of nowhere a wife stiffens in her seat
and looks across the room. There's nothing there,
but still she looks, hoping that the words will fall
from the heavens. There is no easy way
to say it, so she leans into the table
and without apology says she's had enough,
that it's her turn to find herself, that the monotonous
orbit she's been forced into won't do. Her tight, stony fists
hang in her lap. Silences stretch light years,
and all the feeble attempts at reconciliation
will never reach her now. It's the same feeling
as when Mark Preston blind-sided me,
stone-hard knuckles snapped the ridge of my nose,
a stream of blood flared into the parking lot.
Some other kid might have swung back, but I was horrified
at the pool filling my palm. *My blood*,
I repeated to myself as I sat there
quietly while a friend finished off the guy I believed
was trying to finish me. He never knew what hit him.
Nor did Mrs. Hodges until they calmed her, medicated
her from a pain that wouldn't end. Years later she'd wake
to the fiery ache in her leg, a reminder of what she'd
been and what she'd become, survival's gravity
twisting her life into one deep breath, like the first breath

that coughs up the phlegm of another world and deposits
it right here in this one where all around us stars
flare into bits of battered stone, and the universe
leaves each of us alone to explode in all directions.

Why I Believe in Angels

Because I've seen their musculature joined
hip to hip in parked cars, their bones,
under the glisten of skin, twisting into flight.
Because I've seen them rock through one another
in that oldest of nights, in that moonless hour of clarity
when the field mouse briefly turns its head from danger
and only a wing beat marks its passing.

Because I've heard them speak in tongues
in late night bars as their bodies writhed
in the stage's strobed light. Because I've seen
their breasts encircled in the incense of cigarette,
and I've held their heart's beating planchette and deciphered
scribbled prophecies on back-alley walls and discovered
their words, like ours, are mere ticks on a clock.

Because I believe the quark and lepton that leap from lover's mouths
were once part of a rotting branch on Centauri Prime,
and because I wake at night full of a past compressed beside me,
the voices of friends whose wives left or husbands cheated,
who, faced with such truths, are certain they didn't know:
"I stood there," they confess, "though someone else possessed my body."
Then all I can imagine are the unpaid bills a life accumulates,
the voracious guilts and minor misdemeanors, the interpenetration
of morphogenetic fields that allows the rat in Seattle to convey
the way through the maze to a rat in Boston to the rat inside my head,
and because I can't ignore these signs, because I can't ignore,
I find, without looking or understanding, my wife's hands,
or my son's hands, crossed upon my chest,
and there like two wings they've ended their journey.

Tool Box

When he gave me the one his father had
given him, he said, "A good tool invites you
to pick it up." His were hands that held many.
Knew the difference between the weight
and balance of a ratcheting wrench
and a spark plug wrench. His were arms
that lugged power tools, hand tools,
vintage woodworking tools, garden tools,
and a lunch pail of the kind
no one owns anymore. His was
a back bent beneath the labor only men
and women used as tools can know.
Bent in the bean fields and hay fields,
bent by shingles carried up the roofer's
ladder, bent by the concrete mixer,
bent by the sledgehammer and shovel,
the jackhammer, the hoe and spade,
the engine block. His were palms
that knew other palms by their callouses
or lack of callouses. Knew my hands
were hands familiar with keyboards
and ballpoint pens, and understood
those were tools, too. Knew we all
were tools of war and power, tools of lust
and loss, tools that eventually lost
their use, grown weak from age,
rusted from neglect. When he asked me
to help with repairs after a storm,
I knew this was work he could no longer
do alone. I brought the toolbox with me.
I handed him a hammer and waited
to follow his lead as I always had,
knowing sometimes trying is all
that's asked. Sharing the small losses
this tinkering with our hands can almost fix.

Cheerleaders at Forty

They're in love again
with the old language of lunge and kick.
While others rush to work,
they're framed in windows at the local gym
training in Pilates, their children preened
and packed off to school, their husbands, former quarterbacks
and point guards, huddled in insurance office cubicles.
Even now their school girl voices overheard
in grocery stores and shopping malls
could rile the marching band's tight-lipped clarinetists
who hated them, their rouged cheeks,
mascara-lined eyes, their moussed hair,
how each sweater hid little from the crowd,
how they'd bend on hands and knees then rise in pyramids.
Despite the talk, few boys ever loved them
in breath-fogged Fords, desiring them most
haloed by stadium light in late September
before adolescence burned to cinders in factory fires.
Now at the gym they're pedaling stationary bikes,
swimming laps and hovering above ellipticals,
attempts to stop their universe from flying into entropy,
anything to halt the memory of their breath ghosting
in the cold of those Friday nights when the final whistle blew,
and the frost, without warning, began blooming all around them.

Kathleen Nalley

Black Dress

Although your mother cooked
pasta, lasagna, tiramisu,
you weren't allowed to eat
more than three bites,

always a size two, to stay a size two,
always a halved grapefruit
on the counter, pink packets
of Sweet & Low, a bowl of peaches
rinsed of their syrup, fists
measuring perfect portions.

Boyfriends knew to deny you
milkshakes at the Starlight Drive-In,
where high school lovers swarmed
the parking lot, having only a few
hours before fathers would go looking.

You subsisted on Saltines
for weeks before senior prom,
the black dress your mother made
intentionally a size too small,
her tape measure lassoed
around your 21-inch waist.

Now, in the mirror, all you see
is what you never were—
fat and bulge and droop—the last
bobby-socked girl to be asked
to dance. Now, laugh lines
corner your mouth.

Mid-life, you've got wonderfully
open carotids, jeans that fit,
secret cravings and scales
like gargoyles in every room,
watching over the numbers,

those damn numbers that creep
into your sleep, wake you
in a panic, as if you're walking
late to class naked, as if there's
an algebra test you forgot to take.

Behind the louvers in your closet,
the perfect little black dress,
in case someone dies.

Concentric

After the Ringling Brothers Circus, a newborn was found by a janitor in the toilet at the Bilo Center in Greenville, SC, February 4, 2011.

Maybe the plunge from one body
of water into another didn't disturb
you the way we think, that you emerged
quickly, swam even, by instinct, from one
bloody bowl into another, that the only thing
you noticed was the change of temperature—
raging red heat to clear chemical cold. Somehow,
you survived, kept your head up
where your mother had perched you
on top of the toilet seat, somehow knowing
not to let yourself submerge.
Baby John Doe they called you, placed
you, once the janitor blew life
back into your lungs, in a hospital incubator,
tubes feeding nutrients through your nose
to sustain you. Maybe you'll never know how
all this started. You'll never question
how you entered this world:
your mother, a K-Mart customer service rep,
your father, once unknown, now coming
forward to give you a name: Water Bearer,
Aquarius, and you will rise like a tidal wave
onto the earth: first, subsiding
and receding, the undercurrent pulling
you back; then, second, furious.

After the Layoffs

These days, you come home speaking of phlox,
smelling of gardenia, the blood
of roses still on your shirttail.

How I envy your calloused thumb,
green as sun coleus, the perpetual
black curl of dirt in your nailbed.

It's hard to imagine your big biker body,
bald head, tattooed arms, dividing
the tender saplings, nesting them in beds,
perfectly aligning pansies with peonies.
You were bred to nourish,

knowing before frost to prune
the butterfly bush, planting sunburst
sedum under the birch, knowing it
will take and spread and pop
against the patina of copper downspouts,
the weathered cedar shake.

When you were slung from the Rolodex,
cut from the 401k and were told
the cubicle comb was closing, dread
seeded and bred like wisteria
all over our home, those annoying
bees of doubt pollinating the kitchen
every morning, where you kneaded

dough, folding and tucking and turning,
the delicate balance of yeast and salt and air.

Some days, I think of losing everything.

I daydream of slinging hash at a local diner,
where I chat it up with the regulars, offer Fred
a free piece of pie on his birthday, wear a name
like Jill or Jenn or Mary scrolled across hard plastic,
settle my hands on my hips, complain
of grease stains and bunions.

I want to flirt with old men as skinny
as French fries, refill hours by filling
ketchup bottles and wiping counters clean.
And after closing, commune in your
harmony garden, while you snore,
a backfiring muffler, and dream
of fertile soil, the bowing heads of begonias.

In the morning, the flower and flour,
all tended, ready to rise.

Slow Churn

You can take your molecular gastronomy
and shove it. You may call
it "marshmallow caviar," but really,
those little want-to-be roe
are nothing but liquefied sugar
and chemical smoke melded
into tiny spheres of goo. Or your "i-cream,"
whose fast-acting liquid nitrogen
makes instant goodness
in a matter of seconds—you can have it.

I prefer the slow churn, the muscular turn
of a hand crank, the ice crystals
that form themselves in their own time,
the smooth, stiff peaks that fall over in waves.

Give me the good, ol'-fashioned root
vegetable loosened from the dirt
that grew it. Give me beans to snap.

These days, everything is complicated,
bedazzled, soul-stripped. It's all about
bling and feathers. But no matter
how many fake diamonds you superglue
to a dime-store watch, it's still cheap metal
that turns your wrist puke green.

I want nothing to do with the 4-chord
machine-driven, synthesized pop song.
Give me the tensile plunk of a 5-string,
the perfect fever pitch of two siblings weaving
their voices together on a front porch.

Give me the crow's feet circling
my eyes, the thin purple
stretch marks around my thighs,
the battle scars that show I have lived.
No Botox, no Clorox, no washing away
of the dings and stains that truths memorialize.

Sometimes there's nothing better than the feel
of scraping old paint from the windowsill,
of ripping off the bandaid, of saying what
you mean and actually meaning it.

Sure, sometimes it's cool to do it
standing with one leg in the shower and the other
curiously splayed above your head, but really,
whatever became of the missionary position?

The heavy weight of another barely hoisted
on top of you? That slick, sweaty, hard-
to-breathe kind of love where you peel
your sticky bodies from one another when it's over

—it's nasty and you know it's nasty, but it's
the kind of nasty that makes you feel whole—

that puts you back in touch with something primitive
and natural and raw—no pretty pink accoutrements,
no gizmos or gadgets or silver-rimmed handcuffs, but

the thigh-slapping, hair-gripping kind of sincerity
we hate to admit we need —
unfiltered, immediate, and naked.

The '49s

Once ranked 49th in education, S.C. was home to the infamous "Corridor of Shame" due to grossly inadequate school facilities and supplies. Ironically, Gov. Mark Sanford, who used state dollars to fund an adulterous affair in Argentina, fought against federal money to help his state's struggling educational system.

Lapis-blue mountains and
piedmont green, pea-green of salt
coasts and palmetto-green of trees;
there is no gold visible here. There is no
shiny rock, mica, filament, only green and
red clay, red clay packed in between the green
of leaves, red clay in eyebowls,
red clay under nailbeds of those trying
to make things grow, red clay lining
the backs of swollen throats.

We've made it through drought,
cratered and cracked lakebeds whose
fish moved on to better breeding water.
We've made it through sweaty seasons of
mosquitos, crunchy palmetto bugs,
humid breath hovering, sticking to skin
like Saran Wrap over ground beef.

We've made it past water boiled in batches
on cooktops in dusty, sweaty kitchens of
diabetic women smoking,
who raise their children
and then their children's children,
those with grocery-store feet
and hollowed eyes
who can barely read
but can't wait to start
breeding themselves.

Some of us have made it through
schooling in schools without walls,
or at least in schools with holes in walls,
just big enough for rats and
squirrels and the humid air to hold in heat,
with books disregarded
by generations past and passed down

for reading by those with
little instruction, but maybe
because of a little golden gleam
in their eyes, thirsty
for a drop of knowledge, they take
whatever they can get, and once gotten,
feel like they can do something.

Some have made it because of belonging
to a lineage of rich men who
settled on white plantations where
labor was cheap and dark and workable
and because old money took to
the land like beans, was easy to grow
and easier to tend because someone else
was always watering, always
composting the red clay into more fertile soil
where nutrients would break
down the pockets of cash
into something for the next generation.

You do not know the toil of preparing the fields,
the wretched, battered hands of
those who picked cotton
to make your fine button-down-collar
starched shirt, your hands greasy
only from eating ribs. You sprouted in pastures
already readied for harvest. And because,
you look for gold in other places,
where gold on the wrist of the dark-
haired woman lured you to lands
where promise is more alive and
moons are bolder than the crescent sliver.

But, here, in South Carolina, the rains
have finally come and the heat rises and
dirty-handed children sit atop containers
meant for other things, reading leftover
books about people moving to other places
out of want for something better,
the gold underfoot not yet dug up.

ASHLEY M. JONES

ALL Y'ALL REALLY FROM ALABAMA

"...The straitjackets of race prejudice and discrimination do not wear only southern labels. The subtle, psychological technique of the North has approached in its ugliness and victimization of the Negro the outright terror and open brutality of the South."
—Rev. Dr. Martin Luther King Jr., Why We Can't Wait

> this here the cradle of this here nation—everywhere you look, roots run right back south. every vein filled with red dirt, blood, cotton. we the dirty word you spit out your mouth. mason dixon is an imagined line—you can theorize it, or wish it real, but it's the same old ghost—see-through, benign. all y'all from alabama; we the wheel turning cotton to make the nation move. we the scapegoat in a land built from death. no longitude or latitude disproves the truth of founding fathers' sacred oath:
>
>> we hold these truths like dark snuff in our jaw,
>> Black oppression's not happenstance; it's law.

Slurret

You a spade, a spook, an open-mouthed
black pickaninny. Ashy Aunt Jemima,
Americoon, you blue-gummed Beluga,
you cotton-picking jigaboo. You, drenched
in chicken grease, you watermelon head,
you tar-skinned porch monkey, ain't never gonna
get a job, you yes suh shuck and jiver,
you hanging tree baboon—for years, we watched
you bleed beneath our skin-splintering whip,
we watched your eyes embolden, swell like veins.
You turned your begging hands to thick brown fists.
What are you made of? What fabric sustains
its fibers, stays elastic despite rips—
embossed with flame, but a brocade remains.

Love Note: Surely

with first line from Gwendolyn Brooks

Surely you stay my certain own, you stay
obtuse. Surely your kisses were little poisons
gripping tight my lips, my arms, mapping their way
across my unsure body. Surely, this fission

is a gift—a gilded parcel laced like God, scent
of Mother Mary's milkbreath and her virgin promise,
that virginal mirror, me. Surely, I was sent—
and, incidentally, that other *she*, to put you on notice—

hearts aren't toys for juggling, no, the blood
too sticky to really ever disappear—
surely you know that. Surely, your own beating brick withstood
the blows I tried to strike with my unrelenting care.

The morning opens, now, without your sun-blacked face—
the bluejays and morningbirds sing away your waste.

Contralpunctual with Gladys Knight and Infidelity

oh yes

I heard you,

with your top teeth only

Oh yes

the whole grapevine

can hide under a tongue,

it can grow, love

it can speak to me in my sleep—

my eyes are grape leaves, love,

even the birds sing this sour song.

You could have told me yourself.

Am I worthy of love?

oh yes I am

I am afraid to love you,

a man who smiles

hiding something at the bottom.

I heard, love

can fit under the molars

even as it says *love, love, you*

through my ears and down my throat, love,

even as you hold me, love,

covering the most bitter fruit.

I bet you're wondering how I knew—

I wonder, too—

I am

   the grapevine

Photosynthesis

When I was young, my father taught us
how dirt made way for food,
how to turn over soil so it would hold a seed,
an infant bud, how the dark could nurse it
until it broke its green arms out to touch the sun.
In every backyard we've ever had, he made a little garden plot
with room for heirloom tomatoes, corn, carrots,
peppers: jalapeno, bell, and poblano—
okra, eggplant, lemons, collards, broccoli, pole beans,
watermelon, squash, trees filled with fruit and nuts,
brussels sprouts, herbs: basil, mint, parsley, rosemary—
onions, sweet potatoes, cucumber, cantaloupe, cabbage,
oranges, swiss chard and peaches,
sunflowers tall and straightbacked as soldiers,
lantana, amaryllis, echinacea,
pansies and roses and bushes bubbling with hydrangeas.
Every plant with its purpose—
flowers to bring worms and wasps. Even their work matters here.

This is the work we have always known—
pulling food and flowers from a pile of earth.
The difference, now: my father is not a slave,
not a sharecropper. This land is his and so is this garden,
so is this work. The difference is that he owns this labor.
The work of his own hands for his own belly,
for his own children's bellies. We eat because he works.

This is the legacy of his grandmother, my great-granny—
Ollie Mae Harris and her untouchable flower garden.
Just like her hats, her flowerbeds sprouted something special,
plants and colors the neighbors could only dream of.
He was young when he learned that this beauty is built on work—
the cows and the factories in their stomachs,
the fertilizer they spewed out—
the stink that brought such fragrance. What you call waste,
I call power. What you call work I make beautiful again.

In his garden, even problems become energy, beauty—
my father has ended many work days in the backyard,
worries of the firehouse dropping like grain, my father wrist-deep
in soil. I am convinced the earth speaks back to him
as he feeds it—it is a conversational labor, gardening.

The seeds tell him what they will be, the soil tells seeds how to grow,
my father speaks sun and water into the earth,
we hear him, each harvest, his heartbeat sweet, like fruit.

Harriette Winslow and Aunt Rachel Clean Colard Greens on Prime Time Television

In their dollhouse kitchen,
they clean a bouquet
of collards
while the comedy of errors
unfolds around them—
Harriette in her pantsuit and that blackmother

smirk that signals the hard love only a mother
can muster. This, holy kitchen,
culinary sanctuary, covers them
in light, its white glory a bouquet
around their perfect hair. Their fingers know no errors
as they pick and place the collards.

There was an earthy magic in my mother cleaning collards,
their mineral scent, the sink-full of water my mother
plunged them into, the water which washed them of their errors—
greens baptized, clean from sediment and rock, our kitchen
sink her pulpit, the leafy bouquet
her holy book. How we wished we could be them,

touched by our mother's godly hands, then
cleaned so well we forgot they were just collards—
they glistened, a sparkling bouquet
of dinner-yet-to-come, so loved by our mother
that even they forgot their natural bitterness. A kitchen
is sweetened when collards are cooking, the air a

swelling porkfat perfume, the onion's pungent terror
nulled by the ribboned greens—I loved to watch my mother cut them,
roll the piles of flat foliage up like a cigar, the kitchen
knife shining against a tight army of collards.
We needed no superheroes when we had her, a mother
to rival every black mom on cable—no fragrant bouquet

could rival the smell of her greens and cornbread, the bouquet
of cotton swabs and peroxide she'd use to sanitize our playground errors.

She was a magician, more than just another mother—
she could turn an afro into a constellation of braids, adorn them
with a galaxy of beads. She could turn a sprawling batch of collards
into a smooth and savory feast, a world exploding in her small kitchen.

Someday, mother, I will inherit that sweet bouquet
of cocoa butter, Blue Magic, kitchen smoke and calm night air,
the perfume of black motherhood. One day, I will learn how to cook them collards.

GABRIELLE BRANT FREEMAN

LETTERS TO TED ALLEN

Dear Ted,
I've told you all my feel-good stories. Please don't ask
for the ones that will make me cry. I don't want to cry
on camera, and I especially don't want to cry
over this giant gummy anatomical heart
that I haven't even started to melt down yet.
Five minutes have already gone by with me
running around the pantry looking for cornstarch,
for egg yolks, for anything to thicken me up.
I feel I'm on the verge of breaking.

Dear Ted,
I have no idea what to do with chicken hearts and
artichoke hearts and strawberries shaped like hearts and
conversation hearts. And…I'm starting to take
the mystery ingredients personally.
I mean, I know. I knew what I was getting into.
You get candy hearts? Smash them to bits with a meat tenderizer,
stick them in a skillet with butter and alcohol and hope
they stick together. Drink directly from the bottle
until you feel better about not leaving
any single basket ingredient whole.

Dear Ted,
And anyways, if I cry into my bread pudding
made from leftover pizza crust, crushed hearts
of palm, and a cinnamon and sugar prayer, it won't matter
that I baked in this kitchen. Took A. Big. Risk.
The judges won't eat it, won't even push it around
in the presentation-perfect vessels I chose, expose
the still raw centers with their sharp steel tines.

Dear Ted,
That's what happens sometimes
when you put everything on the plate. I know.
I didn't come here for validation. I didn't come here
to prove to myself, to prove to anyone else, that I made
the right decision. But, damn. Ted?
A win here would mean everything.

In the Turn

Van Halen's "Panama" is not at all about Panama.
It's about a race car or a stripper, or a race car and
a stripper, but either way, there's nothing about the country
in the song, and that's appropriate because "Panama"
was released in 1984, the year Orwell wrote we would all
be convinced that what we knew to be true was wrong.

In the bridge, you can hear the throaty twelve cylinder engine
of Eddie Van Halen's 1972 Lamborghini Miura S rev deep.
I spot a Lamborghini on the road and my son thinks I'm cool
for a hot minute. The Miura is named after the line of
Spanish fighting bull bred to fight men armed with lances
in rings studded with humans coveting blood.

Heat comes off of it. And oh, we throw roses.
We throw roses at their feet. I can barely see.

Ferdinand the bull snuffles flowers to his gentle nose, his breath
warm against a girl's hand. Balboa hacks his way up a mountain,
sees an ocean no one he considers to be a person has ever seen before,
claims it all in the name of the Blessed Virgin and King Ferdinand II
of Spain. Claims its discovery, carves a symbol of his religion
into a tree with his conquering sword. Balboa dismantles

entire ships, has them carried across Panama to the Pacific. Re-
assembled. *I own this ocean.* There was no stopping them.
Imagine Balboa explaining ownership to the *caciques. You hold
no power. Bow to your King across the sea.* A man tells his wife
what she remembers is wrong. And isn't your memory bad
anyway? And aren't you aways so emotional? Let's look at this

logically. In 1908, one of Balboa's anchors is found
in the middle of the Panamanian jungle.

An anchor lost in the middle of the jungle is a reminder
of the fact that I dismantled my life and moved. For love. For
you. An anchor in the middle of the jungle is an iron reminder.
You gird yourself in armor. You hold a standard depicting
the Holy Mother high. Wade in the water waist high.
The US expands a railroad built by the French across

the isthmus of Panama. They want to shorten a shipping route,
so they cut across a continent. You want to shorten the argument,
shorten the time it takes to address the problem. Gut
through the subject, wave your shiny cape and jab, jab,
jab until I weaken just enough to believe. You may be right.
The Lamborghini Murciélago is named after a bull whose life was spared

by the matador after surviving twenty-four sword strokes. The wife lives
despite sharp sticks in her back with flags that dance. The key is not to die.

Feruccio Lamborghini began naming his cars after bulls
after touring the Miura ranch, and also he was a Taurus
who are known for being particular and hard working.
My father was a Taurus and particular about things like heirlooms and
cars, and he put bags on planes for 35 years and then he
shot himself in his bathroom with an antique pistol.

From him, I learned how to change the oil and how to change a tire, but not
how to change my course once I started and not how to stand up
for myself and speak my mind. I learned how to drown out my anger with
the roar of an engine and an open road. Murciélago survived,
and sometimes, so does the wife, but not always. 401 years after
Balboa claimed the Pacific Ocean for Spain, the Panama Canal opened.

I have lost my taste for the gradual weakening, for the
quick death. I lower my head. I paw at the ground.

Girltrap

I

This game is a machine involving bowling balls, sipping
birds, boots, babies, bullets, pulleys, and rope.
Begin at the beginning. Measure the natural waist
with tape and a wandering eye. Correct with strings
pulled tight, tug with a foot in the back, make the ratio
deep. Fingers should meet. This game is a machine

involving spandex, stretch, smoothing machination
designed to counter-weight personality, to sip
politely in public, to slip one past calculation
of worth. Numbers matter as much as how much rope
one needs to hang. Measuring tape as noose strung.
This game is a machine involving verbs: to bind. To gird.

Shush of strings laced, waist to hip, waist to bust ratio
slip […] rope smokes. The trick is a boot to the head.

II

Hold her down. It's better if she can't breathe, a waste
of breath. When she faints, waspish, the device
is a couch with a low back. Trigger ligaments.
Her knees will bend, conscious or […] slippage.
Push. Shove. Wrists together and knotted rope,
hoist. This game is a machine involving display, reckoning

salience. Of the feminine. Reckoning
an hourglass, easily turned, manipulated middle.
Hurry up, please. It's time she's waking up, and rope
leaves a mark. If she thinks it's a trick
of her mind. If she thinks she can't remember [slip]
It's better. It's what she gets for […] threads

strung together. Loose. Wasted. Calculate
the number drunk. Insert into machine. Just enough rope.

III

This game is a machine involving knotted strings,
apron and otherwise, and insertion means the ratio
of consent to obligation, degradation, violation slips.
Just lay there. Think of anything else, babies, how waste
products of trees keep you alive, how machines
think. Not how the actual fuck did you get roped

into this. Not how did you swallow the idea of ties
as love, of what it means that man-on-top twists
into missionary, less beast-with-two-backs and more robot,
more hurry up and get it over with, more what is the ratio
of orgasms to daydreams, more […] wonder what your waist
looks like from behind in reverse cowgirl [slip]

and would you have a lasso [slip] braided strings
at your waist […] [Slip] this bit. Into your rebel mouth.

Freak

When you're 13 & U wake up with a body like
that,
your head don't know,
but your body does.
It knows what Prince
is talking about
fuck so pretty
U &
me.
Your body knows strobes, low
lights, a slick ax,
fingertips
slipping up,
up, &
back down
strings tight, stopping here
here
here
mean sex. Yes, sex.
Every note,
sex.
& when you're 13 & U
wake up with a body
like *that*,
they call it danger
& U believe
everything,
buried deep inside your
clothes designed to hide
everything.

When you're 44 & U wake up with a body like
this,
they still call it danger
& every freaking morning U try to fight the urge
to hide
everything:
breasts, waist,
thick hips.

& then Prince comes
on the radio
& reminds U
your body beautiful
is yours,
& it's a fine,
fine instrument.

He starts low,
slow, fingers down, fingers
up inside U,
spreads U open
like a metal zipper unzips
tooth
by tooth.

Presses his mouth
to the mic,
grabs U by your slammin' ass
& grinds
just
like
that.

The Happily Married Woman Boards the Plane

Please don't be witty as hell sitting in the window seat on a six hour flight with a two hour delay on the tarmac, and don't tell stories that make me snort and say "oh you're cute when" without being condescending, and don't look even remotely like Viggo Mortensen or Christian Bale in the *Dark Knight* but not *American Psycho*, 'cause that's creepy. Although I'd prefer creepy on this flight over spending twenty minutes of shushing, tearing up laughter quoting *The Holy Grail* and LOTR, precious, and seriously, if you know what LOTR stands for and you say Samwise Gamgee is your favorite character, I'll ask to change seats. Please be dumb as a bag of hammers. Please don't order Maker's Mark and ask if I'd care for one, too, and then toast to new friends and clink the little bottles and say "clink" and wink at me. Please be wearing sandals and have cracked, yellow toenails, or at the very least please be wearing tennis shoes without socks, or boat shoes without socks. 'Cause then I won't feel like I'm missing something when I pop my earbuds in and start to read the opening to *The Gunslinger*, again. And if I do, don't be polite and let me read and when I get up to use the restroom and come back say, "'The man in black fled across the desert, and the gunslinger followed.' Best line in literature." Or if you do, at least have the courtesy to have obviously profuse body hair, like eyebrows an inch long, visible curly ear hair, back hair flowing across the collar of your *Yo Gabba Gabba!* t-shirt. At the very least, have a fit when the stewardess forgets your second bourbon. Don't you dare say, "It's ok sugar. Would you bring two, pretty please? We're celebrating the discovery of distillation," and then start a conversation on the philosophy behind the end of the *Dark Tower* series, ancient alien theory, or Rushdie's take on hybridity. And god, if you do, throw me a line and, for no apparent reason, say you hate cats, hate your roommates, hate your wife. Or, just say you love your wife and be done with it. Because no matter what the love songs say, I know in six or fifteen years, you'd leave your running shoes on the table *one more time*, your wet towel on the floor; you'd drink the last Diet Coke, eat the very last piece of sourdough bread, and leave me the heel.

Denise Duhamel

How It Will End

We're walking on the boardwalk
but stop when we see a lifeguard and his girlfriend
fighting. We can't hear what they're saying,
but it is as good as a movie. We sit on a bench to find out
how it will end. I can tell by her body language
he's done something really bad. She stands at the bottom
of the ramp that leads to his hut. He tries to walk halfway down
to meet her, but she keeps signaling *don't come closer.*
My husband says, "Boy, he's sure in for it,"
and I say, "He deserves whatever's coming to him."
My husband thinks the lifeguard's cheated, but I think
she's sick of him only working part time
or maybe he forgot to put the rent in the mail.
The lifeguard tries to reach out
and she holds her hand like Diana Ross
when she performed "Stop in the Name of Love."
The red flag that slaps against his station means strong currents.
"She has to just get it out of her system,"
my husband laughs, but I'm not laughing.
I start to coach the girl to leave her no-good lifeguard,
but my husband predicts she'll never leave.
I'm angry at him for seeing glee in their situation
and say, "That's your problem—you think every fight
is funny. You never take her seriously," and he says,
"You never even give the guy a chance and you're always nagging,
so how can he tell the real issues from the nitpicking?"
and I say, "She doesn't nitpick!" and he says, "Oh really?
Maybe he should start recording her tirades," and I say
"Maybe he should help out more," and he says
"Maybe she should be more supportive," and I say
"Do you mean supportive or do you mean support him?"
and my husband says that he's doing the best he can,
that's he's a lifeguard for Christ's sake, and I say
that her job is much harder, that she's a waitress
who works nights carrying heavy trays and is hit on all the time
by creepy tourists and he just sits there most days napping
and listening to "Power 96" and then ooh
he gets to be the big hero blowing his whistle
and running into the water to save beach bunnies who flatter him,

and my husband says it's not as though she's Miss Innocence
and what about the way she flirts, giving free refills
when her boss isn't looking or cutting extra-large pieces of pie
to get bigger tips, oh no she wouldn't do that because she's a saint
and he's the devil, and I say, "I don't know why you can't just admit
he's a jerk," and my husband says, "I don't know why you can't admit
she's a killjoy," and then out of the blue the couple is making up.
The red flag flutters, then hangs limp.
She has her arms around his neck and is crying into his shoulder.
He whisks her up into his hut. We look around, but no one is watching us.

How Much Is This Poem Going to Cost Me?

It's not something I like to burden my readers with as a rule,
the process of spending money for paper and paper clips, pens,
ink cartridges for the printer—never mind the computer itself
which is a whole other story.
                              My favorite uncle
was watching Phil Donahue—the topic was computers I guess—
and a journalist on the panel said, "No writer today
can live without one." My uncle called before the show was over
and offered to buy me my first computer. I dyed my hair red
for the first time, just days before he died. Some readers might think
that might be developed as a separate poem of its own, but since we're all
on tight budgets, I'll try to fit it in here:
                                          How I called all night
and he wouldn't answer his phone. How my sister found him
early the next morning. The tension over his will.
How my mother picked me up at the train station for the funeral,
crying into my shoulder—her dead older brother
who brought her a hula skirt from the South Pacific after the war,
who gave her away at her wedding since their father
had already passed on—before she suddenly got a grip on herself and said:
"What the hell have you done to your hair?" My mother hates redheads
for some reason, always saying she would have drowned her kids
if any of them had been born strawberry blonde or auburn.
When I was little, my uncle used to live in the apartment downstairs.
That was before his wife died, very young,
so they never had a chance to have kids. He told me he felt helpless,
it was like watching a dying little bird…
                                        I pay for this poem in many ways.
Right now, as I write this, I could be at a job earning money
or, at the very least, looking at the help-wanted ads. I could be writing
a screenplay, a novel that would maybe, just maybe, in the end pay for itself.
Sure "there are worse things I could do" as the slutty girl
sings in *Grease*, although it's not politically correct to call her that.
What do people say nowadays? Sexually daring?
I've always liked that character Rizzo—the way she finds out
she's not pregnant after all at the end of the movie,
calling her good news down to her friends
from the highest car on the Ferris wheel.
                                        I wish amusement parks

didn't have such high admission prices. And, of course, I still like
to eat.
    Why just this morning I had a big bowl of cereal. The box says
you can get sixteen servings, but my husband and I never get more than ten,
which makes each serving about forty cents, not including the milk
or the banana or the glass of juice. But without that fuel,
who says I could have written this same poem? It may have been shorter
and even sadder, because I would have had a hunger headache
and not given it my best.
      Then there's rent. I can't write this poem outside
as there are no plugs for my computer, and certainly no
surge protectors. I need to be comfortable--a sweat shirt and sweat pants,
which used to be cheaper before everyone started getting into fitness.
I need my glasses more than ever as I get older.
Without insurance, I don't have to tell you how expensive they are.
I need a pair of warm socks and a place to sleep.
Dreams are very important to poets. I need recreation, escape, Hollywood movies.
You may remember I made reference to one earlier called *Grease*,
lines 32-38 of this very poem.
      It's not easy,
now that movies in New York are eight seventy-five.
You get in the theater and smell the buttered popcorn,
though everyone knows it's not really butter they use.
It's more like yellow-colored lard. Any poet with heart trouble
best skip it. But my husband and I smell it
and out come our wallets. The concession stand uses so much salt
every moviegoer also needs a drink, and everyone knows
what those prices are like. We say goodbye to another twelve bucks,
but that's just the beginning—
there are envelopes, bottles of Wite-Out, stamps, and disks.

On the Occasion of Typing My First Email on a Brand New Phone

When I sign "Denise,"
autocorrect suggests Denise Richards
which makes my ex-husband Charlie Sheen,
which makes me a mother of three daughters,
and sometimes more, as I also volunteer
to take care of the twins
Charlie fathered with his third wife Brooke Mueller
while she's in rehab.
In my new identity, I'm ten years younger,
a lot skinnier, but I haven't read much.
In my new identity, I get breast implants
so I can be in *Wild Things*
for which I become pretty famous
because of a sex scene with Neve Campbell in a pool.
But after that, my acting goes nowhere
except for bit parts and my now-cancelled reality show
It's Complicated, which only runs for a year,
and for which Charlie calls me "greedy and vain."
Sure, I get to be in *The World is Not Enough*,
but *Entertainment Weekly* rates me
the worst Bond Girl of all time.
In my new identity, I still have a sister named Michelle.
I'm still French Canadian, raised Roman Catholic.
I still get to be a writer, but when I'm Denise Richards,
instead of poems, I publish a memoir
The Real Girl Next Door.
I'm a *New York Times* bestseller,
but deep down I know
it's not because I wield a great sentence.
In my new identity, instead of overeating,
I get more plastic surgery and pose for *Playboy*
when my marriage heads south
and I no longer "feel sexy"
and just want to "prove something."
In my new identity, my mother has passed,
but my father is still alive
going to *The Millionaire Matchmaker*

to look for new love. Though I'm no
genius, I'm generally respected
because I don't badmouth anyone,
even when I'm on Howard Stern.
I repeatedly decline to talk
about the restraining order
or any of Sheen's public subsequent meltdowns.
What's the point? Besides, I need to protect my kids.
There aren't many famous Denise's,
and I wonder why my phone, if it's that "smart,"
doesn't suggest Levertov. When I erase Richards,
autocorrect still doesn't recognize who I am.
As I try to re-sign, Samsung asks
if I'm sure I'm just a plain old Denise.
Might I really mean "Denies"
or maybe "Demise?"

Howl

I saw the best minds of my generation (i.e. Fauci, Birx) undermined, doctors hungry for
    truth, dragging themselves through inane press conferences trying to fix the
    prez's anger,
angels with hip replacements and fashionable scarves holding up graphs, making
    predictions, scientific dynamos trying to break through, to give us light,
who, in spite of political tatters and hollow men, sat up Zooming in the virtual darkness
    of cold hard facts floating across cable news hosts' desks, contemplating death
    rates,
who bared their brains to the WHO and saw Monday Night riots, angels staggering in
    Lafayette Square, flash bangs illuminating,
who passed by unimaginative reporters with radiant cool eyes pleading with Americans
    not to drink bleach—tragedy among the non-scholars of pseudo-science,
who were expelled from news conferences by a crazy & obscene Know-Nothing, on
    the whims of a Numbskull,
who cowered in green rooms, undercut, retrieving their speeches from wastebaskets
    and listening to the terrible thump of Trump through the wall,
who got their words twisted, regurgitated, returning to Joe Scarborough with a plan for
    keeping nursing home patients and prisoners safer, flattening the curve in New
    York,
who urged the closing of hotels and theme parks, Paradise Church, shopping malls
    with their mannequins' torsos glowing night after night
with dreams of capitalism, now a waking nightmare of alcohol-wipes, cock and endless
    balls no longer welcome in gentlemen's clubs, strippers shuddering, clouds of
    debt, no spinning on poles, no dollars, Canadian or American, all the motionless
    world of highways with no cars,
Peter Pans playing solitaire on their iPads, plots and more plots dug up in cemeteries,
    drunken, safer-at-home moms and dads banging pans from windows and
    rooftops in honor of first responders who were busy at work, their kids home
    from school, storefronts boarded up, blinking traffic lights, ambulances but not
    much else, sun and moon and tree vibrations in the spring dusks of Minneapolis
    and Louisville and Buffalo, until the protests began, the best minds of the next
    generation chanting, demanding sanity from the worst King America who was
    clearly out of his mind.

Lisa Hase-Jackson

Just

Just now a subtle breeze, a trick of water, a dog's bark
        and another,
        and another.

Just now men with rifles,
        masked reporters,
        a camera.

Just now four rose bushes, a dozen blooms,
        three spent daisies,
        fox fern, blue pot,
        iris.

Just now a rampant virus, a floating ward, a parade of pundits, a jury.

Just now another pie, another pet, another letter
            in the mailbox.

Just now a president.

Just now a row of peas, a mound of squash, a trellis
        of tomatoes, pepper spray.

Just now satire and improv. The news; a president.

Just now the dishes, a flash, the laundry, tall grass,
        a stimulus check.

Just now a woman asleep at night
        in her bed
        in her own home.

Just now the shadow of a cooper's hawk across the yard.
        No squirrels,
        no rabbits. Just now,
this president.

Just now protestors against a chain link fence
                around the White House
                Just   now,
                Black Lives Matter

Just now this book, a movie, a playlist, a distant conversation, run.
                Hulu, Netflix, Sling.

Just now, a president.

Just delivered: groceries, supplements, toiletries, pamphlets, pet food, clothes, medicine, books,
                a speech,
                leaflets
                lies.

Just now a noose, a shot, a decision, a red line, a machine,
                a loose cigarette, a toy,
                a knee to the neck,
                a storefront.

Just now a polar vortex, a verdict, a tropical storm,
                rubber bullets.

Just now, the arctic circle
        one-hundred degrees.
        Sea levels. Just now
a subtle breeze,

a trick of water, a dog's bark
        and another
        and another.

You Find Yourself in Kansas City

among house-proud women
and men who are mean with money

and rent apartment #8, the first
900 sq. ft. you've ever had all to yourself.

You don't mind that it is across from your mother's
where she can keep you close

and at arm's length all at once because
the space is cute – because there is a porch

for plants – and then you find
the HVAC for #8 is unpredictable,

or rather just doesn't work even after the maintenance
man bangs on it with the kind of wrench plumbers use

in a show to convince you he's making repairs
so that all three rooms stretching from west to east

and the tiny bathroom, too, remain forever
inclement. Below, a neighbor whose dog

barks, whose stereo blares, who is surly. Soon
you will discover the mice and buy

crappy wood and wire traps at the hardware store
which you will toss away along with the pinched bodies

of bulging-eyed rodents into the trash receptacle
nearly every day despite the fact that the cat

in #10 visits frequently to hunt, brings you mice before there is sun
to play with atop the covers, a strange kind of breakfast in bed.

Yield

Stonehenge is maintained
with a push mower – the ground's
keeper marching back and forth
in crosshatch strips making
the grass short, even
like a haircut, like a golf
course. This is not
how it looks
when my husband
passes the Phillips-
Norelco through
hair left on my mother's
scalp that the hairdresser
couldn't bring herself
to shave. Little
fluffs of charcoal dust
the planks of the deck
while silent birds watch.
The walnut tree sheds, too,
dropping leaves in early
June. For ten years
we assumed this
a harbinger of the tree's
demise. We've learned
though, that it does
this every year.

33rd and Southwest Trafficway

there were two men knocking on the door that night
when my mother answered the door

two men breaching the door-chain that night
when my mother came to the door

there were two men pushing my mother into the living room
that night because she is so small

two men pushing her into the bedroom that night
my mother's very small

and no one heard the banging
and no one heard the screaming
and no one used the phone that night
to tell the police to hurry

just those two men pushing my mother
pushing her onto our bed

two men saying strange things that night
pushing my mother onto the bed

and when they saw a child that night
pop up from the blankets warm

there were two men surprised that night
in the face of a sleepless child

just two men who stopped that night
in the eyes of a wakened child

and as those two men ran away that night
my mother heard them swear

that those two men didn't know anything that night
about there being a kid

and those two men disappeared onto the streets that night
running from what they did

Shard Studded Floor

I was being reasonable about something,
probably the bills or my right to do something –
I had just recently learned how to do this –
be reasonable, I mean, and it was not
having a very good effect on my husband,
the first one that is. I could feel him seething
with anger because, to him, there was nothing
more infuriating than a woman, especially this woman,
standing her ground. Had I been screaming
he'd have found justification to walk out, find
someplace to drink away the day. But, as I mentioned,
I was being reasonable, and I was doing dishes,
a sanctioned activity, so he had to face himself,
and this was hard. I could feel him staring
at my back just as surely as I could feel heat
coming off the old PD Beckwith every winter morning
after stoking it and I was getting lost in this metaphor
when I heard the sudden pop and explosion
of the fish tank sitting on the kitchen island next to me.
Shards of glass & water rained everywhere. I felt bad
for the three gold fish flopping on the floor of glittering glass,
suffocating in oxygen. I remember now: the children
had overfed the fish, the water grown murky with food,
but what really set him off was that I didn't get excited,
reasoned that the fish tank could be cleaned out, after all.
Somehow, it seemed reasonable to him to throw
the plumber's wrench sitting on the kitchen table
at the five-gallon aquarium in reaction, as if it wasn't obvious,
his ability to overpower, I mean. I scooped up the fish,
tossed them into the fishpond we'd built by the back door
and told the kids to put on their shoes, we were going to town.
I had a little money, I don't know how –so the kids and I
saw two movies back to back at the new theaters in Topeka
that afternoon. First, *Twister,* then *Mission Impossible.*

Junk Mail

My new husband pulls the hood of his sweatshirt
over his head and jokes, in that inappropriate way men

think so funny, that I should come looking for him
if he doesn't return from checking the mail.

My heart jumped that short space between my chest
and throat, but I didn't laugh because it was dark

outside and all of our neighbors are white.
I worried every minute of the five he was gone,

recited the Serenity Prayer five times
before he came back through the front door, keys

in hand, dragging a little of the night's cool air with him.
In the pile of mail, sealed envelopes

from utility companies, a church flier, sheets
of glossy coupons – impossible to recycle.

The evening passed as so many do: dinner,
reading in bed, goodnight kisses. When morning

comes and my husband leaves for work, I watch
him drive out of the cul-de-sac. The sound

of the engine fades into sunrise as I go to the closet
where he hangs the clothes he doesn't fold, pull down

every single hoodie he owns, even the Adidas we bought
in Korea, and shred them all to unwearable strips.

Tyree Daye

When My Mother Had the World on Her Mind, Crickets in Her Ear

1. Boy, don't let a shadow in you, I never want to see the devil in your eyes, a traceable line of your daddy's.
2. If you dream about fish or a river, somebody's pregnant, we need the water more than it needs us.
3. Dream about snakes, you haven't been living right, wash your hands of it.
4. They're shooting boys who look like you. You know my number, use it, keep all your blood.
5. Stay
6. alive.

Ready

In the end crazed
keeping the lights on all hours
like a desperate casino
he called for his dying
hoping it would run out of the night like a primordial dog
renewed from digging up the cemetery soil tracking up his tan house
Old Mo' ungovernable
the city sent him plenty of notices about his junk cars
& offshore drilling tools
from his working days
his sunken in roof
covered with a tarp blue as sky
I come to know his story
from my Uncle Pac
who because he was a man of the lord
took to cutting Old Mo's yard
I learned Old Mo's love for blonde women
how his blended pear & apple wine
could calm the pulse of a rabbit
could change the mood of a snaping turtles' snap
Now he was old and ready to go feathered & ready to fly
thought he'd started something simple that would take him out
like it did his mamma & daddy
quiet as a broken chime as heat lightning he thought the ground even was against him
as it grew every tomato & watermelon seed he'd spit out his window
If he touched a dead bird in the street
it jumped back to its feet & thanked him Old Mo'
full of life
& scared to death

Tamed

I was the unbroken horse
of that town, slept standing up,
held on to the breeze like wildflowers.

I kept caterpillars in jars,
my mama let them go,
I figured they just disappeared.

There are moments you can hear God
say things soft-spoken, the sun
settling between thin pines.

Collected crickets in 2 liter bottles,
dropped them on a path far from the house
one or two at the bottom drowning
in the last swig of cola, the smell of mama's
leaf pile faint and almost gone.

My mama would say
to kill a cricket
is a sin against the night.

Same Oaks, Same Year

My cousin kept me and his little brother
saved me from our uncle's

pit bull, then spent seven years
in prison for his set.

Every other word
he said was *blood*.

      ***

Uncle Nuggie showed us
      how to make a BB rattle
inside a squirrel.

Two small holes,
enter and exit.

All summer I wondered
what leaves the body?

Gin River

If the Neuse River was gin,
we would've drunk to its bottom,

        its two-million-year-old currents alive
        with shad, sunfish, redhorse, yellow lance,

all the blood from the Tuscarora War.

We would have drunk it all,
        aunts and uncles would have led us in Big Bill Broonzy's
        "When I Been Drinking,"

until everything inside us began to dance
and we all joined in,

silt around our ankles,
our footprints on the banks
leading down to the water.

Dirt Cakes

My Grandmother's body
lives under an ash tree
on an old church ground, her spirit
can be seen making
a maple tree's shadow jealous.

The church's bricks absorb the choir's songs,
they flake Holy Ghost,
If Trouble Don't Come Today.

I visit, fall on my knees, ask
her how she doing? How long
is her hair now?

Does she still like it braided
in front? Still like having
her scalp scratched?
What y'all doing
in heaven today?

She'd tell my mama
don't let a bird get the hair that falls
out your head, they'll use it to build a nest
and you'll never leave Rolesville. Dirt

is the only thing I know that can't die,
it makes sense
we would bury here, makes sense
mama don't want me playing in it.

MELISSA DICKSON JACKSON

Ode to the Avocado

Oh—alligator
pod, toad-fist nugget, you
of the green-mealed heart, pimpled, pitted,
glazed organ of densest fuel, husk of lunch
— let me love my fickle self as I love you—
cursed though we are by these imperfect
margins, this spin of skin around a
seeded core, this changeable
flesh, this too brief, this
faultless, peak.

The Mermen of Forsyth Park

> *In Savannah's Forsyth Park, the 1850 Neoclassical Fountain celebrates humankind's industry and dominion over the sea.*

Let us praise the Mermen of Forsyth Park
and their fantastic asses, their shofars jetting
four translucent arcs of plumbed-in city water.

They are white as a blister rising. They are still
as a cataract and blind as time. Praise
that harmony of beard and bicep, of swan

and groin leaf and pelican. Because man
is beautiful. Because man is absurd.
Because there is gold in the hills and oil

in the dale, ships in port, and sailors at sea.
Because we have crossed the wide water
and plundered the jungles, found

our own dust on the desert of the moon,
and shipped our voices into the vast
and wordless beyond. Because

the merman's tail is a story we need
to believe and praise enough
to keep singing our own.

Paper Bird

The house is gone.
And the one before that.
And the one before that.
Still the camellia blooms
In a newly terraced yard.

Drive out toward Primrose.
Lovely Primrose. Each path
Carries the balance of home.
The oak leaf hydrangea
Forsythia, honeysuckle and now
The white knockout.

White brick. Whitewashed clapboard.
White porcelain. A dressing gown.
A piece of chalk. An interrupted
White line. Drive out
Toward Primerose. A flash
That the tub should be caulked.

The steps painted. A vision. Eggs
In the cupboard, a poundcake,
A mixer. A shelf of Corningware.
A white sedan rolls quietly
On the county road still
Unnamed and there in white,
A family intact. Girls

Gathering clover, gathering
Chickweed, gathering coneflower.
The chapel stands. The schoolhouse bell
Rings and the train passes whistling
As it does every day. And you are not

Any more in that hollow, railed,
And lonely bed. And I am not assembling
Words that are not about paper birds
Or wild flowers or the color white.

Diorama

Here is the earth borne down and magnified
through my child's few years: shoe boxes, crayons,
frayed brushes, glue sticks dried up or nibbled away,
a shell from Jekyll Island, a baby food jar.

A third grade science project, in it is fixed
not so much the ghost crab, its habits and habitat,
so otherworldly from my son's, but his own
most mortal and familiar domain.

On this stage, the tiny crab grows colossal,
the abject object of my boy's assigned dilemma,
her infant prey held in flight on party toothpicks.
There is no end to the ghost crab's desire,

her appetite as immeasurable as a mother's worry,
but he's only drawn six hatchlings and the ghost
will have to contend with looming there forever,
glued, as she is, to the diorama's back wall

while the sugar pearls-cum-turtle eggs are buried
in a pint of sand and imagined into a swarm of sorrow.
He's read the crab must devour them lest her species
grow ghostlier yet when the turtles return to nest.

But look how his morning glories rage on the faux dune,
and the clipart clams cluster in a painted wake,
and the sweep of the sea oats whispers sweet reason
into the bay's boxed and ever still wind.

The Humans

Have scattered, have dithered and dathered, the humans
In helmets, in velvet, and veil, the humans recoil to their roosts
With buckles and booze, in funny white shoes,
The humans in duds of charmeuse, in knickers or knit, they scatter

And gather to chitter and chatter. The humans they scatter,
They wave and they whimper the glib and the glibber, scattered
Like feathers or flint. They rumble and riot, roost
In the viaduct, cruel fellas in slippers or boots, shoes

Patent or suede, slacks checkered with jade, shoo
Them home with their cheap chirping hearts, battered they scatter,
The dear pitter patter of boys and girls tumbled and tossed, scattered
Then smattered they swig and they swagger and shoot, shoehorned

And shopworn, the hoodlums and well-born, the humans
All clamor, get fatter and fatter, their brims and their shoe
Leather burst, go home to your harems, your roosts
Ripe with cherubs, you belles and you barons, your shoes

Laced with scarabs, you roosters and hens, you peckers in pens, you scatter
and stammer and flit. The humans, they want and they wane. The humans

Taking the Backroads to the Orthodontist

My son explains how a *Three Musketeers* bar is like bauxite

    which he says is expensive to mine and a nonrenewable resource

but has holes in it like the candy he has to write

    about using at least one analogy or metaphor. "Like bauxite,"

he says, with an outside "slick as clay, the color of mud."

    I draw a cloud in the dashboard dust hoping to suggest

the nougat center is fluffy like a cloud.

    "Nice geode," he says. So I draw a sun and point

to the sky where there are no clouds after all.

    He says, "Mars is a dead planet but full of iron—that's why it's red."

And I wonder if he knows that the *Three Musketeers* he ate

    last night because a boy with braces can't have a *Milky Way*

is made by the Mars company which also makes

    the *Milky Way*. I wonder if he knows how much nougat

looks like bauxite with its sediment of almonds

    and pistachios. Though the *Three Musketeers* nougat

is nothing like that, just whipped chocolate

    with holes, like he said. "Mom?" he asks as we turn in

to Dr. Cranford's where new wires will be tightened

    against his teeth already clad in steel, "Do you understand

   what I mean by Aluminum Ore?" I don't, but I can see

    his assignment coming together: the candy bar,

the planet with its frozen core orbiting just beyond ours,

   the miners in Les Baux scratching

 at the countryside's open sore for nearly 200 years,

  a nonrenewable resource unbound from its wrapper.

"It's like a book you can't judge by its cover," he says.

   Like Alexandre Dumas, his face as plump as a geode,

 his hair like bleached nougat.

David Colodney

Glass

And next week I'll ask you the same question again
even though you told me last week not to always ask
when you'd be home because you *just don't know.*
What I said was *we wanted to know if you'd be here
for dinner* but what I wanted to say was *this is my house,
show some damn respect.* I didn't want to sound
like my own father, voice roughened by the flora
of cigarette butts blooming in his chalice ashtray,
but I was now him, my wine glass
taking the place of his pack of Winston 100s,
having this same talk with a similarly cocky
teenage son oozing the cologne
of braggadocio and bravado.

When you live under my roof, you live by my rules
in my father's day was the gray cliché of parenting
a teenage son, nearly a man in so many ways yet not so
in many others. My father's rules wouldn't work today,
in this brittle era of eggshell words and participation trophies,
so I attempt to tilt my son's fulcrum toward adulthood
by talking in tempered terms instead, knowing the hourglass
offers only so many more next weeks to ask
if he's coming home for dinner,
leery that the wrong words can be as fragile
as shards shattering as the door slams closed.

Turnstiles

This train has a lavatory like an airplane
and uniformed women in red tunics serve
snacks and beer. I close my eyes
and think of those boyhood subway rides
through the Bronx. My father jumped the turnstile
and told me to crawl underneath
to save the 50-cent fare.
I couldn't wait to be tall like my father and hurl
myself over the turnstile, a sort of working class
Olympic event. The turnstiles are different
today, more like revolving doors
with fortified steel gates. My father and his New York
are long gone, lost to America's restless rusting.
My father never left the U.S., even when he served
in the Army. With my eyes still closed I see
him sitting beside me now: on a high-speed train
pumping through the veins of our Italian
homeland with my wife, who sips a Prosecco.
I drink a Peroni while I read Richard Blanco,
and I hear my father's voice asking not *how* we paid
our fare but, rather, *if*.

Passengers

So, mister, you ever make out on a city bus in the driving rain?
        I did ONCE, at 17, riding home from high school,
kissing a friend of my sister who told my sister she liked me.
        Eyes like ravens, bubblicious chewing gum-glossed lips,
she got off at my stop, lived a block over. Two teenagers kissing
        on a bus full of strangers, all sitting staring forward,
transfers held in leathered hands, riding home from jobs
        that left them empty. Two teenagers: the thunder outside
quaking away our inhibitions, precipitation washing away
        the ugliness of a world we hadn't yet discovered was so ugly.
At 17, the olive drab GI Joes we played with as boys are still stored
        in our moms' attics, but we're less than a year from maybe
becoming GI Joes ourselves, sent somewhere we don't know,
        somewhere we can't spell.

So, mister, you ever make out on a city bus in the driving rain
        and never see that person again? At 17, that was ok, because promises
held the weight of circulars rolled through windshield wipers.
        Today, the miles are measured in years and the broken
promises breathe like currency. I sit on a city bus folding bubblegum
        into my mouth and think my own 17-year old son
may be kissing a girl on the city bus he takes home from school,
        two teenagers savoring the surreal landscape of a kiss in traffic,
in downpours that rattle the windows like hip-hop.
        At my stop I leave the newspaper on the seat and open
my umbrella to the clouds, hoping to beat him home, hoping to sweep
        the military recruitment letters that pelt him daily like
hailstorms into the trash before he arrives.

Reserved

I didn't know she smoked cigarettes in the alley behind this office
building, my secretary, with her type-perfect fingers arched over correct letters
on her keyboard, by my side working late stuffing envelopes, pushing pencils,
pretty and young as the night is raw and dangerous. She's in the Air Force reserve.
I thought reserves met a weekend a month to talk shit and drink beer in a uniform.
I didn't know they were a fighting unit, deployed to worlds unknown, whisked
from their families in some muzzle-flash fury. She's seen combat.
My secretary has seen death at her boots. She's camouflage in the desert.
She's 5-feet tall maybe when she sinks in the Iraqi sand and, in the ordinary gunfire
of corporate deadlines, my secretary is hard like mortar, loud like bombs.
When she returns from active duty, a civilian again, I feel I let her down.
Our office has no glory no glamor no twilight's last gleaming. I'm no patriot.
I'm a mannequin and so is she, both plastic against reality and paper for a paycheck.
The tasks I ask her to do must seem so mundane. When she asks for a smoke break
I stand and salute. She's home among the dead cigarette butts scattered
and smoldering in the minefield out back.

Deployed

Your bedroom clock scatters us in minutes.
You rattle off random tasks   chores
before departure: physicals   basic
training storage   lease-breaking.

You already speak staccato
like your drill sergeant, hollow
broken syllables. Standing at attention
we survey these blank walls
pretending: diminished breaths
an open window. A lonely cloud burst

blurs your orders clutched in spastic hands
tearstains   drain white paper gray.
I see through the folded print   an x-ray.
If I touch that letter, it means you're leaving,
so I let angular words   dangle.

In this minute, there's no changing you.

In this room, we live a moment
we don't understand: your bedroom clock
spins time faster   as you ship out to serve
        decaying America.

Young soldier, if your country loomed as large as your heart
beating   under camouflage   last name   embroidered,
flag emblazoned   if only   your country
          appreciated.

In this minute, I don't know: salute you
or hug you so tight
you never go.

Sarah Cooper

Pantoum for Departing

If you're living, consider:
who will autograph your tombstone?
What human will wait 'til you're lowered
and chisel you a love letter in granite?

Who will autograph your tombstone,
she asked me lying in her death bed.
Then, chiseled letters of love with granite teeth
and bit her lips, chewed cheeks.

She asked me, lying in her death bed
if I *had a poem that rhymed,*
and bit her lips, chewed tattered cheeks.
She said she needed, *something to focus on.*

If you had a poem that rhymed
I'd remain respectfully fascinated,
she said. We needed something to focus on.
Needed syncopated sounds.

I'd remain respectfully fascinated
on the rhythm and repetition
of our need for syncopated sounds.
She knows she can't, do this alone.

On rhythm and repetition
what human will wait 'til you're lowered?
She knows she can't do this, alone.
If you're still living, consider.

Centered

Once, I read the heart pumps 2,000 gallons of blood
every day. My mother always had a gallon of milk

in the fridge, She would pour it in thick mason jars
at dinner, over ice. *Milk should be consumed perfectly chilled,*

she would say. Wouldn't drink it any other way,
made me drink two glasses daily as I refused

to be breast fed for the first month of life.
Newborn babies have the fastest heart rate

the pediatrician told my mother. She heard
there's an organ tied to hummingbird wings

in your daughter's thoracic. The tie-dye t-shirt
I wore until someone peeled it from me

smelled of vinegar and indigo: rings punching
across cotton fabric. In fifth grade I learned

an adult heart is the size of a fist and situated
in the middle of one's chest. That felt fitting to remember

when my mom died. She didn't die
from heart cancer, which is rare since heart cells

stop dividing: less room for mutation, for error.
Either way the heart still beats 115,000 times a day.

When mom's stopped mine wanted to sync to hers the way
a horse's heart can mirror a human's. *I don't like*

all these feelings, I finally acknowledge to my doctor.
Your heart can beat outside your chest, he insisted.

I responded, *Then take it out.*

HANDS & MOUTH

I strike a match / to burn sage / bundle smoke circles / in every room / of my silent home / I do / this often / I do it infrequently enough / to forget / to do it / more often / often I'm too busy smacking / I mean striking gum between teeth / When I was fourteen I got braces / for my imperfect smile / for dental health / for other reasons too / my parents couldn't afford them / but wanted my mouth / to smile proud / One Christmas / I drank too much tequila / and said something like Mom / this mouth has afforded / many a woman / many a / pleasure / she maybe said / your tequila tongue lives behind / white / straight teeth / in a queer mouth / your face is striking / either way though / I strike a match / burn sage / hold it to my face / under my nostrils / wave it over / my head / past my shoulders / open a bottle / brace for quivering lips / let her ashes soar / over Stoney Lake / they never strike water / but land / over / quiet ripples.

Hiking with an Erasure Heart after Adrienne Rich's "The Floating Poem, Unnumbered" & years of Emily Dickinson & Sappho

plant some hydrangeas

        no-exchange rate currency

If hope   buy leashes

           things with feathers fly away?

be fair [

              ] earthy things

    wet dirt on boots   calloused hands

  handle, remember: thicketed bones of your torso [

        ] blood pump is

    cylindrical symphonies

    evacuation

serenade space   one's partner

    somewhere else, some colder town

            devour

contours of my pain.

Driving Home

Sun splices through sky of winter
                              slits morning, razors clouds
the way invisible matter hacks (everything).
                              I'm navigating a road I could do
blindfolded but choose to do eyes wide.
                              Tears have a way of forcing one to blink.
The dried blueberry patches, farmed by winter
                              are crisped, tinged with frost.
I remember your hands dyed azure
                              from thick harvest summers
from days spent back bent picking
                              for jam. The stone church
haunts all of us. Some man baptized
                              me there and I don't remember
his name. Pastor. Sir. Reverend.
                              You were not that man. You are whom
I drive home too. I call you Dad, not father
                              not man. Behind your home is a thicket,
a patch of magnolias vining
                              in hand-held harmony. I ran away there once,
actually twice. I took your handkerchief,
                              the red argyle one. You should know that.
You should know I kept it.
                              It's in my desk drawer, the desk you built.

As a carpenter's daughter

she's always thinking
about air around objects,
about how objects stack,
how trust can be material:
Jenga is wooden blocks
of trust and vulnerability.

Here's a story for context: You come over,
walk in the door, talking, won't stop talking
about air filters, double-pane windows,
ways out of the house you're having remodeled.

She wants to tell you
of the dream she had last night.
The one where her mom is alive
from a stem cell treatment,
the one where she knows she is still sick
and will die. Soon. She wakes gasping,
can't inhale, can't wrangle enough air
into her body.

You are still talking
so she swallows subtle gulps
tries to take the air deep into her nostrils,
practices ujjayi, release
through back of throat.
You never notice her doing this,
not today, not any day.

You just said something about windchimes.

JUAN J. MORALES

My Father Looking at Bruegel's *Landscape with The Fall of Icarus*

After my talk in the art gallery,
where I projected images of paintings and ekphrastic poems,
my father walked up to Breugel's landscape
giving me his memory
with skepticism in his voice.
"That one with the plow?
I used to do that, on our land
behind the house in Puerto Rico.
Except it wasn't with a horse.
It was a bull, going forward. I steered.
The little wheel there
would guide the blade into the soil.
Slicing open the field."

He didn't have time for the sea, ship, or northern city
faded into the rocky coast. He kept
working, telling me how,
"I planted the sugar cane.
Drop it in, push the dirt over.
Drop it in, push the dirt over.
Drop it in, push the dirt over."

I entered my father's painting
that understood Icarus' splash
with eyes never looking up
from the field that became humidity
mixed with overgrown decades
when our family's home
gave way to becoming
a kingdom of massive bee hives.

Like a Tired Balloon

After a bad week of standardized testing,
    our English class went outside
    to free balloons
        with attached notes

            that became a message in a bottle,
       swimming through the air.

        When we heard from the woman
          two states over,
              who found one of our notes

        clutched by the tired balloon,
      we were still jaded, but impressed.
We admired how one balloon

could beat back
    elements to escape. The planted seed
              grew into

        the maybe

        we could also fly away

           from our school's octagon of lockers
           and our futures mapped toward
           military or retail. We could float

    into a world bigger
  than our hometown, to discover
    anywhere hopeful wind currents
        might take us.

Dog Eats Hand

If this is the mangled moment
      I become a few fingers
           short, I will stay

        pale as the clouds if I can free
    my hand from

the dog's gaping mouth.

The large dog shakes
      his head to tighten grip. I jab

my fingers down

      his throat.

          My freed hand

              is now held out. It bleeds
        then swells. Puncture wounds open

      memories of me at eight-years-old,

again learning lessons I already know,

about my hand through
      the fence

          to pet a strange dog.
    Shock drops me
    to the street.

The Democracy of John Elway

Back in college days, way after the Cold War,
here in Colorado, where Bronco fans
worship Rocky Mountain sunsets that bleed
the blue and orange,
five buddies, who couldn't afford curtains,
rented out the house and pinned
the massive USSR flag
on the living room wall for everyone to see.
It bathed the room and entire street in revolution red.
The hammer and sickle didn't flinched
at the rock that smashed through their giant window
and the attached note that declared,
"Communism sucks, John Elway Rules!"

Pueblo Boulevard Elegy

It pains me
  to pass three black limos
  and a hearse driving
  directly under
  sixteen vultures
  circling like a welcoming committee
  in blue sky high.

I've had so much ache
  in my back lately.
  My coughing fits
  have me expecting blood.
  The doctor says
  walking pneumonia,
  but I'll survive.

They say, it's going around,
  and I wonder if it could be
  what drives the procession of cars.
  Now in the rearview,
  routed to cemetery gates,
  they are sombra,
  shadowed, first as cough,
  like mine, from days ago
  when the person was still alive.

Every Last Supper

I am writing to understand

The Last Supper

        in every childhood home.

How every kitchen table
        centered
        under the painting, carving, or porcelain

        Christ framed by Apostles,
            en la concina,

near the tiny TV
on top of the fridge.

This is still the backdrop
        for tight Easter and Christmas feasts,
            breakfasts and dinners

between work
        shifts and school

when our mother cooks.

It is the penitent feeling for not
        eating every bite
        of arroz con lentejas,

        and Jesus looking down,

as a relic with opened arms,
        voice whispering,

My flesh. My blood.
Eat while you can, mi hijo.

ZORAIDA ZIGGY PASTOR

Salami and Cucumbers

I am sitting on the countertop
under harsh florescent lights,
in the mustard yellow kitchen of my childhood
while my father digs around the refrigerator.

He is looking for the salami he bought.
He walks over to cabinet,
just above my head.
He pulls out a bright green can of Keebler crackers.

He sets me down on the floor and wipes the countertop clean.
He unwraps the salami like a present.
He opens the can of crackers,
and takes out a package of saltines and places the salami on top.

He gives the first one to me,
like The Lord's Supper at church.
He says, "This is how you eat salami."

He takes a big, greedy bite, so do I.
He lights a cigarette.
Years later, my parents went their separate ways.

Now, I'm standing in a white kitchen
under harsh florescent lights.
My boyfriend is teaching me how to properly slice a cucumber.

He takes out a plastic cutting boarding a
large paring knife.
He says, "Make sure to cut the cucumber like this,
your thumb should always be behind your index finger."

He leaves me to my task of sloppily chopping the cucumbers.
He checks on the fish. "It's ready,"
he says.

Late Night

I was the child who read deep into the night.

My father gave me a tiny red lantern,

the kind you hang on your keychain.

My mother and I shared a room.

We slept on twin beds with

identical floral bedspreads.

My mother would turn off the light.

I would lie awake, waiting.

Finally, I would pull from under a pillow

A discarded purple textbook.

I would read it, under the covers,

I was a hot, sweaty, sticky, kid,

reading the lion, the witch, and the wardrobe,

my tiny lantern, a beacon.

My Mother's Tongue

My mother's tongue is slippery.
She strings together words
in limited broken syllables to make
clumsy sentences strung together
like a child's homemade necklace.
She says to the telemarketer
on the phone, "Anything else."
She meant nothing else.
She doesn't want anything else.
"Not want anything," she says again
and hangs up abruptly.
She tries though.
At work, she says "how you doing my friend?
Happy to see you."
She beams a child's radiant smile.
I am glad we can speak Spanish.
With her broken English,
she strung together a life in exile.
She pledged allegiance to America.
Many nations under one nation,
together, indivisible under God Amen.

You Bring out the Cubana in Me

after Sandra Cisneros

You bring out the Cubana in me,
the olive-skinned Caribbean goddess in me.
The one that loves the salty kiss of
the ocean, the one that
loves to sip prosecco with you.

You bring out the Cubana in me,
La Virgin de La Caridad del Cobre in me.
The very Virgin that guides Cubans
across 90 miles of water
on homemade rafts.

You bring out the Cubana in me,
that raunchy, loud
oyé -chico-que-te-pasa in me.

You bring out the Cubana in me,
the one that is teaching you to like gizo de maiz,
Spanish corn stew of my childhood.

You bring out the Cubana in me,
like it or not, cariño. I will let you
eat in bed, but don't spill a drop of
coffee.

You bring out the Zóraida in me
the bien carbrona—no
comas mireda in me.

You bring out the Cubanita in me.
The one cooking you picadillo from scratch,
chopping onions that burn my eyes and make me
sneeze.

You bring out the Cubana in me.
The "where were you? Why
haven't you called?" in me.

You bring out Cubana in me.
The-your-family-treats-me-differently-

because-there-is-no-Colombian-in-me.
 Or is it just me?

You bring out the Cubana socialite in me.
red nails, and high heels
at your cousin's birthday.
You have 1,000 cousins.

You teach me to:
love the "Cubanhoodness" in me.
You tell me it's the alter ego in me.
You say, "Zoraida, you have multiple personalities."

A proper Americana who doesn't curse at dinner.
A Cubana, chancletera, solariega—dirty jokes and bad words.
"You said comemierda in front of my mom!"
"Sí. ¿y qué? So, what."

You bring out the Cubana in me.
Loud, hands on my hips, moving my
body like I roll my Rs
as I learn to love you,
as I learn to let you love me.

Fire

I.

I am sitting at the bar, alone,
my choice.
The Atlantic Ocean
full of seaweed lies stagnant to my left.
My family is bathing
in that puddle they call the ocean.
It no longer takes me aback.
Ever since he left for the promise of work,
I am so often, deliriously, alone.
I am reading *The Great Fires* by Jack Gilbert.

The poet is burning,
his body alight, aflame.
Love, he says,
is one of many great fires.
It lasts by not lasting.
The poet is burning
for the love of his departed Michiko.
Upon her death,
he searches for her hair,
all through their house.
I, too, am burning.
I, too, am burning for: love—
his love, his scent of sweat
and cologne. It is the scent of our home.

II.
Home—torn from us,
running to a distant land,

running out of space,
like this notebook,
running out of pages.
The story has been told or not.

My great-grandfather jumped
in front of a bus,
they said, he was unable to live with
The fire of loss
What was his name?
Loss is our story.
Forgetting is a fire
that burns
deeper and deeper, still.

III.
Lost our bodega,
Lost our hardware store,
loss is our story.
I am an immigrant's daughter
reaching the end
of this notebook.
I have nothing but fire.
No property to call my own.
Just fire, fire, fire
and this notebook
aflame.

Richard Tillinghast

I Tuned Up Seán's Guitar

for Thomas Lynch

I tuned up Seán's guitar
         and gave it an airing
                 on the flagged forecourt outside Lynch's house,
the wind whipping off the North Atlantic
                  three fields from where
  Clare drops into the sea.

Soon I had it ringing
             with songs of my own country,
green mountains, bottomless rivers, deep valleys
    dark as a dungeon and damp as the dew.

I shot a man in Reno, I sang,
            just to watch him die.
                       I had no fiddle to liven it.

The foal's whiteness was something not of this world.
Not till tomorrow would she feel
      on her coat, that was new as anything,
  what we call rain.
Camilla licked the foal's
      leaf-like ears
as I sang out those dire things
  that happened *ten years ago on a cold dark night.*

Even the black crow left off cawing
        when he heard about the long black veil and the
night wind that moans
             and the living who weep over gravestones.
What business had I
      singing into those still-damp ears
ballads of murder and horseback journeys,
   duels and scaffolds
            from a country she had never heard of?

It was some comfort to know
she and I shared no common tongue.

The Boar

That bristly motherfucker.
I'd run out and yell at him
when he came into the yard—
him and the sow and the seven piglets.
I threw rocks
and made a big noise.
But he was not inclined to flee.

As I made a move toward him
trying to look menacing,
he set his trotters into the ground
and feinted back,
more sudden than me.
I could see him thinking, "Come on, take me on
if you've got the balls for it,
tall two-legged animal
with whatever that is you're wearing on your head.
See these tusks?"

So Barry the pig guy came, set his snares
on the pig-trail through the *hau* trees
and trapped him.
"What the fuck!" the boar bellowed,
"I have absolute right here!
"I forbid this!"

Barry lassoed the pig and bound him
hind legs and front,
dragged him squealing out of the thicket.
That fellow would go to the pit.

But the cry that boar let loose
as he struggled against the ropes,
split the peaceful sky of our hilltop.

The chickens ran under the house,
dogs barked in houses half a mile away.

And God knows what the baby goats next door
made of it.
Nobody had told them yet
about borders and killing and rage.

BLUE IF ONLY I COULD TELL YOU

Homage to Garcia Lorca

       1.

Blue if only I could tell you
      how much I love you blue.
When I buy ink it's you I go looking for.
Even before the sky turns blue and
  I get out of bed and pull on my levis
I sail my gaze out
     over turquoise and ultramarine,
salt breeze and leagues of ocean.

       2.

Not Officer, he beat me up blue,
not His fingernails are turning blue.
    I fill my pen with königsblau,
      listening to Miles and
vanishing into the inkwell's unfathomable O.
     I sniff the breeze for direction,
minding the tilt of swells and the tide's mood swings
      hearing dolphins chatter
        as they launch up from the depths.

       3.

Shakespeare, in that movie they made about him,
  his fingers, whenever the camera let you
      see his hands,
         were blue with ink,
even when he shimmied up
      the rich girl's father's palace wall.
This was the hand that wrote
     The lights burn blue, it is now
    dead midnight.
        In the clouds *a towered citadel,*
a pendent rock, a forked mountain or blue promontory—
    white and azure,
      laced with blue of heaven's own tinct.

4.

Do you remember your first set of oils?
Cobalt like Hokusai's *Great Wave of Kanagawa*
or the underside of a Winslow Homer swell
        in a storm off Barbados,
the sharks beside themselves with anticipation,
        rolling like dogs.
Aquamarine like a summer morning in Laguna.
  And the tube of Navy like World War II,
victory at sea taking off from steel-gray carriers
and men in blue pinstripes
        who made their fortunes off munitions.

5.

Is it hard sometimes to know just who you are?
Green shimmers to the east of you, purple to the west.
        From the lapis of your earrings
comes the resonance of temple bells
        above Kathmandu.
In the sapphires on your bracelets I hear
        the sounding whales,
  singing from the depths of their longing.

Or

Finned or on the wing
Rooted or foot propelled

Dressed to the nines
or Salvation Army free box

Plays well with others
or out there on your own

Sent from God
or look what the cat dragged in

Barbered and nails done
or picking fleas from your scalp

Golden slippers
or sneakers patched with duct tape

5G
or two tin cans and a length of string

Hanging on your every word
or shut the fuck up

Clueless
or elementary my dear Watson

The wind at your back
or ain't nothin' workin'

Lungs filling with air for your first cry
or refrigerated, a name tag on your big toe.

Took My Diamond to the Pawnshop

    Neuron pathways overgrown
with forgetting and remembering—
        brambles and vegetative junk,
   meanderings and dead ends.

I'm wading through muck,
     scraping silt off
  antiquities that bob to the surface.

•

Let's hose this down and
                      see what sparkles.

•

A map of the Pacific
                walks by on a man's t-shirt.
A pear falls.
   The wind blows away my pages.

I followed my dream
and ended up sleeping on the floor,
      thousands of pesos in debt.
Three in the morning and I've never been so cold.

How many times can you land on your feet
      before your feet get sore?

Leavetaking

Of course it was raining
when I stepped outside
        on the little porch,
naked except for a towel.

Greenness lit up the morning.
        Redwing blackbirds
piped in the rushes at the lakeshore.

  Outside, the car awaited,
my belongings inexpertly packed.

Other cars move in my direction,
domestic creatures only.

Rain pings on the windshield,

        the moment of indecision
folded like a handkerchief
        in my back pocket.

Julie Marie Wade

Atlantic Elegy

We see a little farther now and a little farther still—C.D. Wright

*

I ask the rain to remit, but not because I am ungrateful
A raincheck for the rain—is such a thing possible?

In Florida, even the cold is warm by comparison
We sit at the ocean's lip as it licks the sand from our toes

Consider *instead*—the terrifying beauty of alternative

*

I ask the sun to pumice our faces, blind us humble and good
Incumbent sun, so long accustomed to winning the stars' wars

Consider *although*—like trying to whistle with a mouth full of Saltines

We only know what we know
We only see what we see

*

I ask the space to persist after the hyphen that separates
Birth from death, to leave the parenthesis like a gap tooth

Then to no one in particular, I say: *What age is not a tender age?*

*

This hapless haptic misses her Blackberry
Such tender buttons, were they not?
The tiny Underwood slick inside her pocket

*

I ask the lifeguard not to hang the purple flag
For jellyfish and sting rays and the *floating terror*

Imagine if that were your name!

Also answers to: *bluebottle, Physalia physalis, man-of-war*

                              *

Consider *except*—Luminara of a word—bag of sand with a light inside
Synonym for *human* perhaps?

                              *

I am not opposed to the idea of being lost—

Like the red balloon, Mylar with a silver underside—
Buoyed along these stubby waves

Consider *forever*—which is a trick command

A seagull tugs the string of the beached balloon
You see it more clearly now: a webbed design, the visage of Spiderman

                              *

When the rain comes, it is warm kisses, little white beads

Grown-ups stick their tongues out like children do
It's not over till it's over—and then, too soon

In Perpetuity, I Shall Remain the Question My Parents Guess Wrong on *Jeopardy!*

Bellingham, Washington; February 24, 2014

There is snow on the road, which some might consider an omen. Not us. Not after two years of Florida swelter, of longing to be colder, of liking at least a *suggestion* of winter. Ice on the windowsills. Frost on the grass. A shiver sharp as good luck.

We wear black dresses. Not so fancy we couldn't wear them again—though we haven't. We carry bright flowers from the Farmer's Market, arranged by your sister into bouquets we won't toss until the next day—and then, only over our shoulders, only into the Bay.

How strange it was to write where our parents were born in order to procure the license—to have to print their names on that form at all. A narrative altered but never erased. A lineage notarized into law by one county clerk or another. No true new beginnings. And what if we lied or didn't know or refused to remember—would we be denied our right to wed, again?

But here is the sun recusing itself from the day, and here the upper room of Le Chat Noir, flooded with errant light. Here are eleven friends assembled—one officiating, one reading a poem, another signing as witness to the speaking of vows, the sharing of rings, and two little girls playing pretend-wedding afterwards while no one rushes in to say what our mothers always said—*girls can't marry other girls!* They said this often, with words and without them, the complex machinery of their speech and silence, the fields they plowed deep in us, so the dream of this day was impossibly furrowed. Our fathers, who denied such dreams could exist.

We do not smash cake into each other's mouths or toss garters to a flock of eager groomsmen. There are no groomsmen, and no bridesmaids either, which means no one is singled out for being single or dubbed a "matron" because she has already signed on a dotted line, given herself to another.

I am not thinking of my parents' house two hours south of here, or of their other house at the shore, the one I have never seen. I am not thinking of the weathervane on their roof that announces THE WADES live here, or of the elephantine hedges that swell along their borders, in order to mask the fence that masks the yard. The contradiction in terms: declaring themselves, then hiding. I am not even thinking of the difference between secrecy and privacy, which was once explained to me as the difference between what we carry as shame and what we keep for ourselves as an act of self-respect.

I was not ashamed, and yet I cannot believe it was self-respect that compelled me once, from the post office in this very town, to make six photocopies of my thesis—that first collection of lesbian love poems— and then to address six manila envelopes with such meticulous script to the residences of their most cherished friends. "Your mother had to give up her clubs because of you!" my father chided through the phone. "You shamed her in front of everyone!" And though it was my right to claim my love, I regret I ever once used love to punish someone else, even if it was my mother, who could not love the woman I had become.

No, I am not thinking of them as we cross the threshold into our room at The Chrysalis, a grand hotel for which they were breaking ground just as we moved away. But if I were, I would send a small blessing to my parents watching *Jeopardy*! in one of their homes, eating popcorn and drinking Shasta (diet, of course), my mother impassioned as she calls out, "What is Burma, Alex?" and "What is the Prime Meridian?"

I am not thinking of them, though, or how even if they knew I had just married my true love on their side of the country, neither would have found the—*what would you call it, Alex?—the wherewithal?*—to come.

What Date Rape and Gay Marriage Have in Common

It's the making something smaller, see. Shrinking it, paring it down. It's the less-than symbol disguised as simple adjective, trying to upgrade from coach to compound noun: Date Rape < Rape. Gay Marriage < Marriage.

<

It's the Pinocchio Complex, see. Not quite as real as *Rape,* not quite as real as *Marriage.* Synthetic somehow, highly sanitized: surely not flesh and blood, not here and now. Surely not a real-life boy-and-girl, (boy-and-boy, (girl-and-girl…doing God knows what to each other.

It can happen so many ways, *for better or worse, for richer or poorer…* All these possible permutations are likely to trip us up. We need our rapists in back woods and dark alleys, stocking-capped strangers rising out of the fog. We need our weddings in churches, a 1:1 ratio of skirts to suits, bouquets to boutonnieres. We need to know the thing we know isn't really something else, so we call it less-than, see.

<

Do you remember what our math teachers said about the way the parted lips should face? The smaller opening toward the larger, toward the thing of greater weight? Mine said to think of it like Pac-Man eating pac-dots, which are small blips inside a blue maze, easy enough to consume.

So the mouth is always eating that which comes after it, making it less than it was before. The way date is taking a bite out of rape, taking a bite out of crime. (Take that, McGruff. The way some marriages are whittled down like old wood—valid Here-But-Not-There, There-But-Not-Here. (Mythical, in some places, as Atlantis.

Date Rape < Rape. Gay Marriage < Marriage.

<

But what will we tell the children, the fraternities, the county clerks, the beer distributors? What reparations will be made to Vera Wang and Jose Cuervo? Will there be white space on the docket or the Christmas card?

Think of the things we'll have to think of that we never thought of before. Like when the "stewardess" became a "flight attendant" and stopped wearing pantyhose. Order a Clamato juice and sip on that for a while. Does it take you back? Think of all the parentheses we'll never remember to close.

))))

Psalm in the Spirit of an Inaugural Poem

America, I'm going to make you a mixtape, so you'll remember who you are: late nights when you're out rambling across the jacquard landscape of your no longer youth in a 1969 Chevrolet Camaro with black racing stripe or the Dodge Charger your dad loaned you that you better bring back in better shape than you found it—washed with the garden hose, dried with a chamois, whitewalls sparkling where you rubbed each Brillo pad down to a nub—or the bright blue Pontiac Bubbletop you saved up three summers to buy, yet still it stalls out at every intersection: There's the national anthem, of course, and your eyes always grow wide and wet at ball games, even though half the time you forget to take off your cap, forget to splay your paint-splattered palm across your drum-rolling heart, and to be perfectly honest, you're not sure you ever learned all the words to that song: something perilous, something gleaming, and what was that about the ramparts? What parts exactly are those? More so, if you saw the original manuscript with lyrics penned by Francis Scott Key, you'd see how all the full stops are actually question marks, as if even he couldn't be certain that this was really the land of the free and the home of the brave. America, I've seen your lottery tickets and love connections, your tinfoil swans and your Wheaties boxes. America, I know you like the back of my own hand that never learned to drive stick, always popping the clutch of another get-rich-quick scheme, pyramid or Ponzi. But you like the sound of a "star-spangled" something, don't you? Sibilance, so sweet and pure. In this nation of riffs and new renditions, remember when CCR crooned, *Some folks inherit star-spangled eyes*? They were speaking for you and the millions like you: *I ain't no senator's son, I ain't no fortunate one*. First question on the mini-marquee of your game show history, neon lights and three doors to choose from: Who does this remind you of? *Some folks are born silver spoon in hand, Lord, don't they help themselves, oh, But when the taxman comes to the door, Lord, the house looks like a rummage sale.* You're no millionaire's son, America, but you just elected one, and there's some reckoning to be done. Don't be cowed now, don't be fooled: you aren't post-truth, and you aren't post-trauma either. *You got a fast car,* my birthplace, my home; *maybe together we can get somewhere.* Tracy Chapman wrote you a ballad some years back, but I think you had the volume turned down. Then, she wrote you a fight song that you weren't quite ready to hear. Be honest, America, who does this remind you of? *Talkin' bout a revolution,* which *sounds like a whisper* until they get a white man miked; then, it sounds like a roar. Too cynical for your taste perhaps? Land of the souped-up, land of the spoiler, land of singing along with abandon as if you wrote every song all by yourself. Let's try this: Your first inaugural poet wrote, *the best way out is always through,* then glanced sidelong for a trap door or a check-cashing store before he continued: *And I agree to that, or in so far As that I can see no way out but through.* America, this means you, and this means me, too. I'm going to stack track after track of old Spirituals on this tape because we are not done talking about slavery, and at the rate we're going, I'm afraid no chariot will ever swing low to claim us. Hear me now. Stop revving your engine; stop pretending you didn't see anyone stranded out there, flagging you down in the rearview. *Lay Down, Body. Go Down, Moses. Deep Down in my Heart,* America, I think you want to stop gripping that steering wheel so hard. I think you want to surrender the contents of your glove box, too. Looking for amnesty, my fractured nation? You should start by facing yourself in the rust-rimmed mirror in the all-night commode of your friendly neighborhood truck stop. Don't assume that the faucet will run, that the toilet will flush. Don't assume anything at all, America. Didn't your mother teach you "to assume makes an ass out of u and me"? And while we're on the subject, stop flashing your high beams for everyone else to move over. Stop calling "Shotgun!" when taking a ride because half the people who hear you are going to drop to their knees, hands in the air, mistaking slang for warning, confusing plea with threat. *Steal Away and Pray. Study War No More. Will the Circle Be Unbroken.* You're scaring me, America, taking the turns too fast, pushing the needle too far. It's plain to see you're in love with your lore, with all your best stories set to music. What can I say? I'm in love with them, too. But it's not enough to roar off into the sunset in your little red corvette, with your pink carnation and your pick-up truck, past every billboard for the Betsy Ross Dress for Less and the Chick-fil-A Closed on Sundays, Yasmine Bleeth in her sheer white swimsuit still asking if you've got milk and the red "H" burning bright as coal on topless mountain highways in the Heart of it All: HELL IS REAL, the sign says. Like you, America, it's perilous and gleaming. But what about the ramparts? What parts exactly are those? *I Want to Be Ready. I Shall Not Be Moved. I've Been a Listenin All Right Long.* Tell me you're made of more than pleather and AstroTurf, my country 'tis of thee, more than apple pie and planned obsolescence, more even than Monday Night Football where we are still *dreaming of heroes*, another poet wrote, where, despite concussions and common sense, men still *gallop terribly against each other's bodies*—perilous, and yet, also gleaming. A friend once told me, "No poem ever saved anybody," but songs are poems, too, aren't they? Surely a song has saved somebody, somewhere. *Amazing Grace*? Turn off the A/C and buzz down your windows, my birthplace, my broken home. There may not be a single answer blowin' in the wind, but hear how the old questions boomerang back, sometimes smashing a window—*How many years can a mountain exist Before it's washed to the sea? Yes, 'n' how many years can some people exist Before they're allowed to be free?* America, smell the fresh air and the diesel fuel, the wild flowers sweet and the wild fires raging. This is our heritage. This, all: the perilous and the gleaming and the ramparts, too.

From the Redwood Forest to the Gulf Stream Waters. From Main Street to Wall Street, as our politicians like to say. Remember that we still have the B-side to write, America. Tie a string around your finger in case you think you might forget. Set a timer on the kitchen stove. In 1999, *Time Magazine* named "Strange Fruit" the twentieth century's quintessential song. Tell me you know this story? It's about a Jewish teacher named Abel Meeropol who "was disturbed at the continuation of racism in America." In response to a photograph of a lynching, which he couldn't cast out of his mind, Meeropol wrote a poem and later set it to music. So the poem became a song, and the song landed in the golden throat of a Black singer named Billie Holiday, who cast it wide as a net with her voice, wide as the oceans that hold us on either side: *Pastoral scene of the gallant South, the bulging eyes and the twisted mouth, Scent of magnolia sweet and fresh, And the sudden smell of burning flesh!* America, this is your heritage, this, all: the lynching and the photograph that preserves the memory of it, our capacity for violence and our fear of forgetting what we have done; also, the man who was moved to write the poem that became this song; and also, and more so, the woman who found the power in her lungs and the vision in her voice to send it out to all of us, *en masse*: strange fruit that never had any business dangling from those trees but now, nearly a century later, because of her, because of him, cannot be unseen and will not go unheard. America, listen: We can't let you take another little piece of our hearts. Now is not the time for lullabies, not the hour to put us to sleep. Yet we can't retreat into silence either. America, America, resist the myth that your greatest days are already behind you. Strike the secret chord we've all been waiting for. Lean in close now and whisper, *like a revolution,* what this century's fierce, sweet, unforgettable anthem will be.

Gary Jackson

After the Reading

a woman walked up and asked how

the young Black poet the month before
could shake with such anger during

his reading. Is it really
that bad? It can't be that bad,
can it?

I told her it was
and she said,

Maybe for you

in Kansas, but here in Charleston
a nice Black man held the door open
for me and my friends
because people respect each other here
and those things you write about
don't happen anymore.

I live here, too, I reminded her.
And by here I meant the world,

but she was already off and talking
about some professor that was

B-L-A-C-K Black,
not Black like you,
and when I was in college in the '70s,
I couldn't understand why on earth
he would come here to teach
in a state where people just don't see
that kind of Black.

The woman pouring wine at the reception
exchanged a look with me —

each of us with arched brows
asking the other,
You believe this shit?

Then another woman
tried to help, said,

It doesn't matter what color anyone is
as long as you're willing to listen
to one another's experience—
but those young people who identify
as different genders are beyond me.

I must have been in a goddamn sitcom
when yet another well-meaning woman
realized they were all starting to look bad
and tried to shut the whole thing down:

Let's talk about the art on the walls,
how good it is to host such a diverse
lineup of poets, how everything's
always been this awful,

but it's getting. Isn't it
getting better?

Elegy that was already done before

I'm trying to teach these kids about elegy when one of them asks *how do you grieve?* Everyone answers: crying, screaming in the crook of your elbow, trying to muffle your soul when all you doing is making it harder for the dead to hear what you have to say. Only one student says *drink*. I put one toe in and ask *what?* He says *Jack Daniels b/c I don't have to think* and now I'm thinking about ghosts again. Last month I talked to your mother on the phone. My mother wanted to show her my book but ain't that like rubbing it in someone's face that one of us is gone and the other got famous for it? Yet here we are—you still dead, and I'm a fool to think the last poem was the last one I'd write about you. At parties, people who don't know that too much ash sours the soil ask about you. I bury two fingers in my temple—one fingernail buried under skin, the other not far behind. Everything is about loss. About stories, about superheroes, about trying to show these motherfucking students what an elegy is really about. It's about the student who asked *who's your favorite superhero?* and I said Spider-Man when I should have said you.

Homecoming

I'm searching the used section. November
whips another flyer in the window
advertising Another Average Brass Band
playing at The Granada. A couple hurries inside
jacketed in leather, collars flipped up;
the bookish clerk mumbles hello
& everything feels like the season

has never changed. I pick up Camus,
a to-do list falls on dust & pine,
demanding: *potatoes & salt,
dry-cleaned clothes, a paper
on Sisyphus, sex with Ryan.*
The sun goes down right
on time. I smile too long

as the clerk gives me my change
& bags the beat-up copy of *The Death
of Captain Marvel*. Outside, the cold
slides a knife in my bones
& wakes me like it should
any creature. *Get used to it*
I hiss between teeth, bite the frost
from my lip. If I could, I'd devour
the winter, this city, every prairie
& flint hill, every star & leaping
synapse demanding to remember

the dog's stupid look, the countless
phone calls I made, the service
studded with strangers wondering
why I wasn't there, but shit—
I'm here now, ain't I? With another
day to kill, another bar to hit
before heading out tomorrow,
this comic my only souvenir.

Fiat Lux

The first moon will be mostly experimental, but the three moons in 2022 will be the real deal with great civic and commercial potential.

> —Wu Chunfeng, chairman of Chengdu Aerospace Science and Technology Microelectronics System Research Institute

Imagine the moon times two, times four, times several times more until there's a moon for every country: all that wonderful moonlight filling parking lots and lonely street corners, and how we'll love it at first and wonder what, exactly, powers each moon, and how did we secure all the moons in place? When we look up, how many lights are stars, or just us staring back? We give them names: Luna Lovegood, Beyoncé, Doris Day. We know it's pointless: finding faces in our newborn lunar bodies: craterless and vast, snow white and smooth: our new favorite things.

Graduation

My thighs are sore from the mechanical
bull I was forced to ride for photo-op
for aunts & uncles, cousins too young

to recall the meal, the gaudy décor,
my *YEEEEHAW* as all the white girls applaud
before they're back to serving drinks,

clearing plates with bits of bone & taking
the check my mother's new man pays
with a few bills, making nice with family

he's only just met. I trade a smile
with my mother across the table—
surprised at my loneliness

without her. The sun sings through Tanqueray
half-empty back at my apartment.
Her man says *straight* & we step

onto the rotting balcony & clink.
It's not competition, but he tells her
he puts it down. She replies

he gets it honest—a little proud,
a little hurt. I pour another drink.
Years from now she'll tell me how

he got locked up & the things
he did when the liquor
got to feeling too good—

if I'd known, I would've tried
to put my hands on him. Instead,
I'm shamed by how mothers

always protect their sons. *You
a booksmart nigga,* he said
on the balcony. *You'll get far.*

We toast. My mother nods,
all smiles with no glass. I pour
another drink to celebrate.

You can't write poetry about things that happened a week ago

one of my students tells me / during a class exercise / it's not a statement / but one of those half-questions they sometimes ask / wondering / if I'll reaffirm or challenge / their still-blossoming understanding / of what they can / cannot do / any event will do / take for example / when evil Captain America picks up Thor's hammer / the crowd goes wild / with rage / how can the newly-christened fascist / nazi / hydra / hate-monger / be worthy / be righteous / imagine 1941 / Captain America socks the Führer / Captain America tosses his shield / through nazi death machines / Captain America's on the front line in Normandy / America liberates the POWs / the camps / America comes home / to parades and comic strips / America's frozen in ice / America / thaws out / America socks Iron Man / America body slams the Red Skull / Hitler's clone / America fights / the war on terror / America cleans up the debris / America points his red mesh glove towards the next jaw to punch / America's fighting the good fight / America dies / comes back / will be / great again / America patrols the border / America tosses his shield / America stops the terrorists / America stops the plane / America forgets his name / America hails hydra / like magic / America turns / America socks Iron Man / America kills / America doesn't want you to know / America wants a secret empire / America's gonna make record sales / America is just what you thought he was / would be / could be again / America happened a week ago / America was never your favorite hero

Acknowledgements

Claire Bateman:
"The Index of Dead Brides" and "A Pocket Introduction to Our Universe" first published
    in *Coronology* (Etruscan Press, 2010)
"The Sinking of the Library" published in in *Scape*, (New Issues, 2016)

Suzanne Cleary:
"Dubbing Room," "Elm Street," and "Sausage Candle" first published in *Crude Angel*
    (BkMk Press 2018)
"Cheese-of-the-Month Club," "Asking for Breakfast," and "Pascal's Wager" first
    published in *Beauty Mark* (BkMk Press 2013)

David Colodney:
"Reserved" first published in *The Chaffin Journal*
"Glass" first published in *Cathexis Northwest Press*
"Passengers," "Deployed," and "Turnstiles" first published in *Causeway Lit Mag*

Sarah Cooper:
"Pantoum for Departing" first published in *Adanna*
"Centered" first published in *Iron Horse Review*
"Hands & Mouth" first published in *Lunch Ticket*
"Hiking with an Erasure Heart/after Adrienne Rich's "The Floating Poem,
    Unnumbered"/ & years of Emily Dickinson/& Sappho" first published in *Lunch*

Tyree Daye:
"When My Mother Had the World on Her Mind, Crickets in Her Ear," "Tamed,"
    "Same Oaks, Same Year," "Gin River," and "Dirt Cakes" first published in
    American Poetry Review

Denise Duhamel:
"How It Will End" first published in *Blowout* (University of Pittsburgh Press, 2013)
"How Much Is This Poem Going To Cost Me?" first published in *Queen for a Day:
    Selected and New Poems* (University of Pittsburgh Press, 2001)
"On The Occasion of Typing My First Email on a Brand New Phone" first published
    in *Scald* (University of Pittsburgh Press, 2017)
"Egg Rolls" first published in *Two and Two* (University of Pittsburgh Press, 2005)
"Howl" first published in *Second Story* (University of Pittsburgh Press, 2021)

Gabrielle Brant Freeman:
"In the Turn" first published in *The Rumpus*
"Girltrap" first published in *Scoundrel Time*
"Letters to Ted Allen" and "Freak" first published in *Barrelhouse*
"The Happily Married Woman Boards the Plane" first published in *Gabby*

Albert Goldbarth:
"Shawl" first published in *The Kitchen Sink: New and Selected Poems, 1972-2007* (Graywolf Press, 2009)
"The Craft Lecture to the Creative Writers of the Low-Residency Program at Yadda Yadda University, with a Late Assist from Wallace Stevens, Robert Frost, Maxine Kumin, Sir Thomas Browne, and Allusion to the Title of an Early Book of Jorie Graham's" first published in *To Be Read in 500 Years: Poems* (Graywolf Press, 2009)

Lisa M. Hase-Jackson:
"You Find Yourself in Kansas City" first published in *Willawaw Journal*
"Junk Mail," "33rd and Southwest Trafficway," and "Shard Studdes Floor" first published in *Flint & Fire* (The Word Works, 2019)

Gary Jackson:
"After the Reading" first published in *The Sun*
"You Can't Write Poetry About Things That Happened a Week Ago" first published online as part of the *Heartland! Poetry of Love, Resistance, and Solidarity*
"Elegy that was Already Done Before" first published in *Tuesday; An Art Project* #11

Melissa Dickson Jackson:
"Diorama" first published in *The Cumberland River Review*
"The Humans" first published in *Shenandoah*
"Ode to the Avocado" first published in *Vinegar and Char: Verse from the Southern Foodways Alliance,* edited by Sandra Beasley, University of Georgia Press
"Taking the Backroads to the Orthodontist" first published in *Southern Humanities Review*

Ashley M. Jones:
"Slurret" and "Harriette Winslow and Aunt Rachel Clean Collard Greens on Prime Time Television" first published in *dark // thing* (Pleiades Press, 2019)
" All Y'all Really From Alabama," "Contrapuntal with Gladys Knight and Infidelity," "Photosynthesis," and "Love Note: Surely" first published in *REPARATIONS NOW!* (Hub City Press, 2021)

Dorianne Laux:
"Lord Of The Flies" first published in *Rattle*
"Honeymoon" first published in *Tin House*
"Joy" first published in *Plume*
"If It Weren't For Bad Ideas, I'd Have No Ideas At All" first published in *What Saves Us: Poems of Empathy and Outrage in the Age of Trump* (Curbstone Books, 2019)

Rick Mulkey:
"Cheese" and "Hunger Ghazal" first published in *Ravenous: New & Selected Poems* (Serving House Books, 2014)
"Cured," "Cheerleaders at Forty," and "Tool Box" first published in *All These Hungers* (Brick Road Poetry Pr. 2021)
"Blind-Sided" and "Why I Believe in Angels" first published in *Toward Any Darkness*

(Word Press 2007)

Kathleen Nalley:
"Black Dress" and "After the Layoffs" first published in *Nesting Doll* (Stepping Stones Press, 2013)
"Concentric" first published in *NightOwl*
"Slow Churn" first published in *American Sycamore* (Finishing Line Press, 2015)

Richard Tillinghast:
"I Tuned Up Seán's Guitar" first published in *Poetry Ireland Review*
"The Boar" and "Or" first published in *American Journal of Poetry*
"Blue If Only I Could Tell You" first published in *Salamagundi*
"Took My Diamond to the Pawnshop" first published in *DMQ Review*
"Leavetaking" first published in *Hudson Review*

Julie Marie Wade:
"Atlantic Elegy" first published in the *Academy of American Poets Poem-a-Day Series*
"In Perpetuity I Shall Remain the Question My Parents Guess Wrong on *Jeopardy!*" and "What Date Rape and Gay Marriage Have in Common" first published *Same-Sexy Marriage: A Novella in Poems* (A Midsummer Night's Press, 2018).
"Psalm in the Spirit of an Inaugural Poem" was first published in *The Rumpus* "Inagural Poems" web series

Contributors

Claire Bateman (visiting writer) is the author of WONDERS OF THE INVISIBLE WORLD forthcoming from 42 Miles Books, and eight other poetry books: SCAPE (New Issues Poetry & Prose, 2016), LOCALS (Serving House Books, 2012), CORONOLOGY (Etruscan Press, 2010), LEAP (New Issues, 2005), CLUMSY (New Issues Poetry & Prose, 2003), FRICTION (Eighth Mountain Poetry Prize, 1998), AT THE FUNERAL OF THE ETHER (Ninety-Six Press, 1998), and THE BICYCLE SLOW RACE (Wesleyan University Press, 1991). She has been awarded Individual Artist Fellowships from the National Endowment for the Arts, the Tennessee Arts Commission, and the Surdna Foundation, and has received the New Millennium Writing Award (twice) and two Pushcart Prizes. She has taught at the Greenville Fine Arts Center, Clemson University and various workshops and conferences, including Bread Loaf and the Bloch Island Poetry Festival. She is also a visual artist.

In *Women's Review of Books* poet Judith Vollmer describes the voice of **Suzanne Cleary** (faculty) as "elegant, discursive, and tough." Cleary's fourth book, *Crude Angel* (BkMk Press 2018), was Finalist for the Paterson Poetry Prize and the Kessler Award. *Beauty Mark* (BkMk 2013) won the John Ciardi Prize for Poetry. Two earlier books were published by Carnegie Mellon UP, *Keeping Time* (2002) and *Trick Pear* (2007). Her other awards include a Pushcart Prize, the Cecil Hemley Memorial Award of the Poetry Society of America, a fellowship from the New York Foundation for the Arts, and residencies at Yaddo and MacDowell. Her publication credits include the journals *The Atlantic, Poetry London,* and *Georgia Review,* and anthologies including *Best American Poetry*. She first came to Converse College as winner of the 2008 Julia Peterkin Award. Her website is <www.suzanneclearypoet.com>

David Colodney (alum) realized at an early age that he had no athletic ability whatsoever, so he turned his attention to writing about sports instead of attempting to play them, covering everything from high school flag football to major league baseball for *The Miami Herald* and *The Tampa Tribune*. David is the author of the chapbook, *Mimeograph* (Finishing Line Press, 2020). He earned an MFA at Converse College and holds an MA from Nova Southeastern University. David's poetry has or will appear in a variety of journals including *South Carolina Review, Panoply, Cathexis Northwest Press, and The Chaffin Journal*. He lives in Boynton Beach, Florida with his wife, three sons, and golden retriever.

Canadian-American poet **Sarah Cooper** (alum) holds an MFA in poetry. Her poems appear in *Lunch, Room, Iron Horse* and other journals and anthologies. Her chapbook, *Permanent Marker*, was released in spring 2020.

Tyree Daye (faculty) is a poet from Youngsville, North Carolina, and a Teaching Assistant Professor at UNC-Chapel Hill. He is the author of two poetry collections *River Hymns* (a

2017 APR/Honickman First Book Prize winner) and *Cardinal* (Copper Canyon Press 2020). Daye is a Cave Canem fellow. Daye has won the 2019 Palm Beach Poetry Festival Langston Hughes Fellowship, 2019 Diana and Simon Raab Writer-In-Residence at UC Santa Barbara, and is a 2019 Kate Tufts Finalist. Daye most recently was awarded a 2019 Whiting Writers Award.

Denise Duhamel (visiting writer) is the author, most recently, of *Second Story* (Pittsburgh, 2021). Her other titles include *Scald; Blowout; Ka-Ching!; Two and Two; Queen for a Day: Selected and New Poems; The Star-Spangled Banner;* and *Kinky*. She and Maureen Seaton have co-authored four collections, the most recent of which is *CAPRICE (Collaborations: Collected, Uncollected, and New)* (Sibling Rivalry Press, 2015). And she and Julie Marie Wade co-authored *The Unrhymables: Collaborations in Prose* (Noctuary Press, 2019). She is a Distinguished University Professor in the MFA program at Florida International University in Miami.

Gabrielle Brant Freeman (alum) is an award-winning poet, an artist, a professor at East Carolina University, and a mom of two. Her poetry has been published or is forthcoming in many journals, including *Barrelhouse, The Rumpus, Scoundrel Time, Shenandoah, storySouth,* and *Waxwing*. She was nominated for a Pushcart in 2017, for multiple Best of the Net awards, and she won the 2015 Randall Jarrell Competition. Press 53 published her book, *When She Was Bad*, in 2016. Gabrielle's art has been shown most recently at the Center for Visual Artists in Greensboro, NC, and as a one-woman show titled *Taking Up Space* in the Faulkner Gallery at East Carolina University in Greenville, NC. Read her poetry and view her work at http://gabriellebrantfreeman.squarespace.com/.

Albert Goldbarth (writer-in-residence) has been publishing poetry collections of note for forty-five years—two of which have received the National Book Critics Circle Award. Individual poems have appeared in hundreds of periodicals from *The New Yorker* and *The New York Times Magazine* to *Kayak* and *Clown War*. His work has appeared in numerous anthologies, including *The Penguin Anthology of 20th Century American Poetry* and multiple appearances in *The Best American Poetry* series and *The Pushcart Prize*. A recipient of fellowships from the National Endowment for the Arts, the Guggenheim Foundation, and the Poetry Foundation, he lives in Wichita, Kansas. This is how old he is: Rick Mulkey was one of his students.

Lisa M. Hase-Jackson (alum) is the author of *Flint & Fire,* winner of 2019 Hilary Tham Capital Collection Series and published by The Works. A full-time writer, Lisa is Editor in Chief for *South 85 Journal* and founding editor of *Zingara Poetry Review*.

Born and raised in Topeka, Kansas, **Gary Jackson** (visiting writer) is the author of the poetry collection *Missing You, Metropolis*, which received the 2009 Cave Canem Poetry Prize. His poems have appeared in numerous journals including *Callaloo, Los Angeles Review of Books,* and *The Sun*. He is an associate professor at the College of Charleston.

Melissa Dickson Jackson (alum) teaches writing and literature at the University of West Georgia. She coedited *Stone, River, Sky: An Anthology of Georgia Poems* for Negative Capability Press. She has published two collections: *Cameo* and *Sweet Aegis: Medusa Poems*.

Ashley M. Jones (faculty) holds an MFA in Poetry from Florida International University, and she is the author of *Magic City Gospel* (Hub City Press 2017), *dark / / thing* (Pleiades Press 2019), and *REPARATIONS NOW!* (Hub City Press 2021). Her poetry has earned several awards, including the Rona Jaffe Foundation Writers Award, the Silver Medal in the Independent Publishers Book Awards, the Lena-Miles Wever Todd Prize for Poetry, a Literature Fellowship from the Alabama State Council on the Arts, the Lucille Clifton Poetry Prize, and the Lucille Clifton Legacy Award. Her poems and essays appear in or are forthcoming at *CNN, The Oxford American, Origins Journal, The Quarry by Split This Rock*, Obsidian, and many others. She teaches at the Alabama School of Fine Arts, she co-directs PEN Birmingham, and she is the founding director of the Magic City Poetry Festival.

Pulitzer Prize finalist **Dorianne Laux**'s most recent collection is *Only As The Day Is Long: New and Selected* (W. W. Norton). She is also author of *The Book of Men*, winner of the Paterson Poetry Prize and *Facts about the Moon*, winner of the Oregon Book Award. She teaches poetry at North Carolina State and Pacific University. In 2020, Laux was elected a Chancellor of the Academy of American Poets. She is also a visiting writer at the Converse MFA program.

Lilith Mae McFarlin (alum) is a poet and librarian from Little Rock, Arkansas. Her first book, *So Long and Thank You for all the Waterproof Mascara* is now available from Sibling Rivalry Press. She enjoys spending time with her parrot and tending to her succulents.

Juan J. Morales (visiting writer) is the son of an Ecuadorian mother and Puerto Rican father. He is the author of three poetry collections, including *The Handyman's Guide to End Times*, winner of the 2019 International Latino Book Award. Recent poems have appeared in *Poetry, The Laurel Review, Breakbeats Vol. 4 LatiNEXT, Dear America, Pank, Verse Daily, Poetry Daily, Crazyhorse*, and elsewhere. He is a CantoMundo Fellow, a Macondo Fellow, the Editor/Publisher of Pilgrimage Press, and Professor and Department Chair of English & World Languages at Colorado State University-Pueblo.

Rick Mulkey (faculty) is the author of six collections including *Ravenous: New & Selected Poems, Toward Any Darkness, Before the Age of Reason, Bluefield Breakdown*, and, most recently, *All These Hungers* (Brick Road Poetry Press 2021). His work appears in the anthologies *American Poetry: the Next Generation, The Southern Poetry Anthology: Volume I and Volume II*, and *A Millennial Sampler of South Carolina Poetry*, among others. His awards include the Hawthornden Fellowship for Writing, the Charles Angoff Award from *The Literary Review*, and the Gearhart Poetry Prize from *Southeast Review*. Mulkey is director and co-founder of the Low Residency MFA at Converse.

Kathleen Nalley (alum) is the author of the award-winning prose poetry collection, *Gutterflower*, as well as the poetry chapbooks *Nesting Doll* and *American*

Sycamore. Written in Dirt, a re-iteration of *Gutterflower,* is forthcoming from Sable Books. Her poetry has appeared in several anthologies, as well as in *New Flash Fiction Review, Slipstream, The Bitter Southerner, StorySouth,* and elsewhere. She has most recently collaborated with a fellow Converse MFA alum on a book-length work that witnesses the intersection of domestic/interior and national/community lives during the pandemic. She holds an MFA from Converse College, serves on the board of the Emrys Foundation, is a frequent contributor to several regional magazines, and teaches literature and writing at Clemson University.

Zoraida Ziggy Pastor (alum) is the daughter of Cuban exiles. While completing her bachelor's degrees at Florida International University, Zoraida was part of the Everglades Wilderness Writing Expedition, where local, aspiring writers learned and wrote about Everglades National Park. Her Everglades themed poems were exhibited at the Ernest F. Coe Visitor Center in the park. Zoraida's work has also been published in the international, bilingual magazine *Mango La Revista,* based in Cali, Colombia. She was featured in Z Publishing House, Best Emerging Writers of Florida two years in a row. She is the author of "Bear Echoes," a poetry chapbook sponsored by O, Miami and The Knight Foundation. She is an active, published member of the South Florida Writer's Association. Zoraida has a Master of Fine Arts in Poetry graduate of Converse College. She worked as a production assistant and researcher for two documentaries on the Panama Canal that are available on Netflix. Currently, Zoraida is a professor at Miami-Dade College.

Richard Tillinghast (faculty) grew up in Memphis and studied writing with Andrew Lytle at Sewanee and Robert Lowell at Harvard. The author of seventeen books of poetry and creative nonfiction, he has held the Amy Lowell Traveling Poetry Fellowship, received grants from the Guggenheim Foundation and the National Endowment for the Arts, the British Council and the Irish Arts Council, has taught at Harvard, Berkeley, the University of Michigan, and is a member of the Core Faculty in the Converse MFA program. His poems have appeared in *The New Yorker, The Atlantic, Paris Review,* the *American Poetry* Review, *The Best American Poetry, The Best of Irish Poetry,* and elsewhere. His 2000 book, *Six Mile Mountain,* is being reprinted by StoryLine/RedHen. He is a founder and past Director of the Bear River Writers' Conference in Northern Michigan and has had residencies at Yaddo and the Millay Colony. Richard currently divides his time between Hawaii and Tennessee.

Born in Seattle in 1979, **Julie Marie Wade** (visiting writer) studied creative writing at Western Washington University, the University of Pittsburgh, and the University of Louisville, and now she teaches in the creative writing program at Florida International University in Miami. Julie has published 12 collections of poetry and prose, most recently the book-length lyric essay, *Just an Ordinary Woman Breathing* (The Ohio State University Press, 2020) and the hybrid-forms chapbook, *P*R*I*D*E* (VCFA/Hunger Mountain, 2020). A winner of the Marie Alexander Poetry Series and the Lambda Literary Award for Lesbian Memoir, she makes her home in Dania Beach with her spouse Angie Griffin and their two cats.

www.ingramcontent.com/pod-product-compliance
Lightning Source LLC
Chambersburg PA
CBHW051559110426
42742CB00045B/3497